D1562872

Eyes Wide Open

Love Yourself & Love Your Body in 9-Weeks

Special Edition

Kimberly Davidson

Contents

Foreword   5

Heal Your Hungry Heart   7

The Dopamine Made Me Do It!   11

Healing Essentials   15

Pre-Study Self-Reflective Exercise   19

Week 1: Pursue Perfection God's Way   21

Week 2: Why Do I Hurt?   41

Week 3: The Beauty of Truth   55

Week 4: Anger Is a Choice   73

Week 5: Freedom through Forgiveness   85

Week 6: Choosing Self-Discovery over Control   105

Week 7: Heal for Life   121

Week 8: Nourish and Nurture God's Temple   133

Week 9: The Road to Damascus   145

Appendix A: I Feel Chart   159

Appendix B: I Want an Eternal Relationship with Jesus!   161

Appendix C: How to Write a Powerful Testimony   163

Notes   167

Please Note

This 9-week program was designed by women for women. Author Kimberly Davidson and Rae Lynn DeAngelis, founder of *Living in Truth Ministries*, have both found true and lasting freedom through the Great Physician Jesus Christ, and are passionate to help you do the same.

This book, *Eyes Wide Open*, coincides with the healing group program, *Eyes Wide Open*, developed by Living in Truth Ministries and Crossroads Church.

This study is not intended to take the place of medical or psychological care. This study is the spiritual component of a comprehensive care plan. Licensed clinical counselors are trained to treat the difficulties associated with emotional pain. *Know when to seek professional help.* Consider seeking pastoral or therapeutic help if your emotions seem out of control and cause you to do things you regret.

While mental health professionals can provide good medical and psychological treatment, *God's treatment on a spiritual level is critical to recovery.* If we allow Him, God will work with our desires for healing to move us in the direction He has already planned for us.

If you ever feel suicidal, seek help immediately. Call 1-800-273-8255 or 911. Ask for help. A professional will provide a safe place for you to talk and tend to your immediate needs.

> "Jesus was the light to a very dark world. He boldly declared that only with God's help could people reach their full potential."
> –Dr. H. Norman Wright

Foreword

I've spent the last thirty years of my life working with those struggling with an eating disorder. Often, it's difficult for them to put into words what they're feeling and fearing. So, it is important when a book comes along with an authentic voice of one who has emerged whole from the struggle. Kimberly Davidson speaks with such a voice. With the help of a dedicated, courageous group of women, Kimberly has tested these materials. Real people, with real struggles, have worked through these pages and provided input, insight, and inspiration.

This is a structured book, designed to provide a pathway along the recovery journey, without dictating every individual step. She knows that, just as each person is different, each journey will be different, and allows the reader to find their own line along the path.

It's also a book of accountability. There is no pretense here. Her chapters are pointed and poignant. For example, she really captures the importance of having a plan to renew your mind as an essential part of recovery. It captures the essence of Romans 12:2, *"Do not conform any longer to the pattern of this world, but be transformed by the renewing of your mind. Then you will be able to test and approve what God's will is—his good, pleasing and perfect will."* Through these pages, Kimberly takes you on a journey of mind, spirit, and body renewal.

Week 5, Freedom through Forgiveness, is a powerful key to keep the reader headed in the right direction through the twists and turns of recovery. As a professional eating disorder specialist, I know the power and freedom possible when a person breaks through to forgiveness. Though the concept of forgiveness is often misunderstood, Kimberly beautifully weaves its thread throughout this book.

Woven also throughout this book is an emphasis and reliance upon God's word. Kimberly recognizes how powerful it is when God speaks truth into our lives and allows us to understand and truly believe it does apply to us. These are more than just refrigerator verses for Kimberly—they are the Words of Life and her desire is to share them with others.

This is a book of truth. Moreover, it's a book of hope. Kimberly has opened up her life and her journey to recovery, not to shout about what she has done, but to celebrate what God has done. The good news of this book is that God can do the same for you. Take the steps. Put aside the strongholds of fear. Embrace what Kimberly has so diligently put together. You will be blessed.

Dr. Gregory L. Jantz, Edmonds, Washington
CEO of The Center for Counseling & Health Resources, Edmonds, WA
Author of *Hope, Help and Healing for Eating Disorders*

Heal Your Hungry Heart

How many of your recent conversations have been about food, dieting, body size, or exercise? Too many to count? There is one common obsession women have: to lose weight quickly with the least possible physical activity and pain required.

From movies and television to magazines and online advertisements, it's impossible *not* to be bombarded by messages and images glorifying the unattainable skinny bikini body. When you're told repeatedly that you're not good enough unless you lose 20 pounds, you start to believe it. I did. In this culture, the pressure to shed fat—at any cost, and the compulsion to compare our bodies to models and celebrities is great.

Did you know you don't have to be anorexic, bulimic, or a compulsive overeater to be an emotional eater? While millions of people are struggling with diagnosable eating disorders, many more are trapped in a "disordered" eating pattern. If you're on a roller coaster with food, dieting, exercise, weight and body size, or are just an occasional binger or purger, then keep reading.

Typically, *emotional eating disorder* means that a pattern of disorderly eating develops. For instance, a person may jump from one fad diet to another without ever stabilizing her weight or learning healthy eating habits. She typically learns to use food to soothe uncomfortable emotions.

A negative body image is just one aspect of the problem. Food is not the real problem either. Unhealthy eating behaviors and addictions get their nourishment from feeding off our God-given needs and desires for love, acceptance, and dignity. There are many causes. Major life changes can trigger an eating disorder. Emotional eating is complex and may require psychological, medical, and nutritional treatment. The healing process can be long and hard, and some professionals contend that emotional eating disorders are not curable. This doesn't have to hold for you. I've seen God heal the wounds of food addiction and negative body image that man thought could never be healed. As the angel said, *"For nothing is impossible with God"* (Luke 1:37).

I found a better way to live, and you can too. The choice to "come out" and change was mine, but the actual transformation was something God did in me. You don't have to be held captive. You're not alone in your struggle and pain. Once you realize the magnitude of God's love, it will build up your self-image and confidence. You can receive a new life and experience spiritual peace, joy, and contentment. *This is hope and the key to healing.*

Second Chances: The Author's Story

An insatiable monster crept into my life unnoticed. Seventeen years old, I lost 15-pounds by following a food plan and counting calories. I looked terrific and received compliments and praise. I wanted more. My body size became an obsession. Soon after, bulimia became my choice of weight control when I figured out I could eat everything I wanted and still lose weight. Immediately, my life spiraled out of control.

Deep down, I knew I needed help. Too ashamed to ask, I chose to read multitudes of self-help books. I worked in the healthcare field and gleaned as much medical information as I could. But nothing worked. An invisible monster had taken control. Then I met God and came to understand I couldn't take my life back without being empowered by Him to give me consistent strength, love, and truthfulness. I also learned that God wasn't going to intrude on my will. He gave me the gift of choice. If I wanted His power in my life, I had to ask for it ... and really want it.

The Bible says we have to make a choice: to walk with God and become dependent on Him, or not. I chose God over this invisible monster. He took me on a journey through the Bible and started to mend me— spiritually, physically, emotionally, and relationally.

God gradually started changing me from the inside out. He spiritually implanted a new heart and new spirit in me (Ezekiel 36:26). As I overcame my shame and fearfulness, my self-image and worth began to improve. I discovered truth. I healed. I recovered.

As a Christian I define *recovery* as, "a process of transformation through which individuals improve their health and wellness, live a Christ-directed life, and strive to recover God's plan for their lives." There are no shortcuts. God can heal us but we still must develop our own life skills and take in spiritual food in order to grow and heal.

God told me through His Word (the text of the Bible is referred to as *Scripture* or *God's Word*) that I'm a beautiful, loved, one-of-a-kind woman. Unlike what the pop culture presents, the Bible *always* tells the truth. God gave me exactly what I needed, when I needed it. I no longer live in bondage because in His Son, Jesus Christ, bondage is destroyed! Today I look in the mirror and I see FAT, a different kind of FAT—*Faithful And True* to my Lord.

"God, you did everything you promised, and I'm thanking you with all my heart. You pulled me from the brink of death, my feet from the cliff-edge of doom" (Psalm 56:12–13, MSG).

The Anchor of Hope

In this book, I honestly share my painful experiences and my heart so we might connect; as well as integrate my education and experience as a pastoral counselor and spiritual development coach. Chances are you will recognize in many ways my story and emotions are also yours—the shame and the transparency, the battles and the triumphs. I believe if a person has hope then anything's possible!

Hope—it's easy to pour caustic acid on hope because then we're not required to feel the pain when our expectations aren't met. If I have no expectations, then I don't have to deal with any kind of loss. The problem is we literally push life away, and God, when we push away hope.

Hebrews 6:19 says, *"We have this hope as an anchor for the soul, firm and secure."* The anchor was a popular symbol in the early church. Those people didn't put their trust in material things or mankind. They put it in their spiritual anchor, Jesus Christ. If we don't anchor ourselves in Him, then by default, we'll anchor ourselves in other people and stuff. God said,

"Cursed is the one who trusts in man, who depends on flesh for his strength and whose heart turns away from the LORD. He [She] will be like a bush in the wastelands; he [she] will not see prosperity when it comes. He [She] will dwell in the parched places of the desert, in a salt land where no one lives" (Jeremiah 17:5-6).

Hope anchored to the goodness and love of God will remain grounded. God's sole desire is to reach into the darkest crevices of your wounded soul and turn your life upside down because that's where you'll truly discover Him. He'll free your heart, mind, and soul so you can love Him and grab ahold of life—of hope and joy and peace. I urge you to put down your anchor of hope. *Something spectacular is about to happen!*

"Blessed is the man [woman] *who trusts in the LORD, whose confidence is in him. He will be like a tree planted by the water that sends out its roots by the stream. It* [she] *does not fear when heat comes; its leaves are always green. It has no worries in a year of drought and never fails to bear fruit" (Jeremiah 17:7-8).*

The Dopamine Made Me Do It!

"**G**et out of my way! I need my fix of cupcakes!"

Ever had cupcake withdrawal? It's a battlefield out there. Scripture says, *"All food is good, but it can turn bad if you use it badly" (Romans 14:20, MSG)*. It's hard not to be addicted to something. The pull is powerful. Why does giving it up hurt so much? I'm not a scientist so I'll give you the "Food Addiction for Dummies" version.

If you eat a *hyperpalatable* food —sugary, starchy, fatty or salty food, the brain releases a chemical called *dopamine*. Most people walk away satisfied. But for some the desire to repeat the pleasure is too strong to resist. Neurotransmitters are responsible for inducing euphoria. One of them is *dopamine*. This chemical fires up the brain when we do something exciting or rewarding. It produces a feeling of exhilaration or pleasure—the "I've got to have it" feeling. We get immediate gratification and find our favorite thing hard to give up, which is a good definition of addiction.

When God created the dopamine response it was for survival. Activities like eating, drinking, engaging in sex, and working, contribute to the survival of the human race. Therefore, our brains are programmed to encourage these behaviors by making them highly pleasurable (see Ecclesiastes 2:24-25).

Is sugar as addictive as heroin or cocaine? Is a cupcake comparable to 'crack' to a susceptible brain? According to scientific data food products can hijack the reward system in much the same way as drugs do. Dr. Nora Volkow, head of the National Institute on Drug Abuse, said, "When a person is addicted, they get conditioned like Pavlovian dogs." Ninety percent of the dopamine neurons in the *ventral tegmental area* of the brain become stimulated when we prepare to eat. The more dopamine released, the more the person wants the food. Addiction develops when dopamine continually floods the brain. Eventually, it takes more and more food to feel normal. This explains why it's more difficult to stop after a couple bites.

Most people, however, don't see food addiction akin to substance abuse. Not only do drugs and alcohol alter brain chemistry, but so do the wrong foods. Speaking about "cravings," Dr. Volkow claims that when people are exposed to their favorite foods but not allowed to eat them, a tidal wave of dopamine surges. They hungered for their food fixes, yet they weren't hungry at all. This is similar to what occurs in the brains of drug abusers after they watch a video of people using cocaine.[1]

Food can act on the brain as an addictive substance. Certain constituents of food, sugar in particular, may hijack the brain and override will, judgment and personal responsibility. Animal studies reveal that hyperpalatable diets, sweet ones in particular, are more rewarding—and potentially more addictive—than intravenous cocaine and heroin. Dr. Mark Gold, chief of addiction medicine, McKnight Brain Institute, University of Florida, stated, *food addiction* is "eating despite the consequences, being preoccupied with food, feeling guilty about your eating habits, and overeating in the face of various health concerns."[2]

Does this strike a nerve? Yes. This book is for you! How do you know if you're addicted to food or something else? Do you feel out of control? If you try to stop what does it feel like? Hell? Withdrawing from sugar produces the same symptoms as withdrawing from a chemical.

Behind every craving is a compelling urge to pursue pleasure—to feel terrific while avoiding pain, physically and emotionally. The problem isn't with having cravings, but rather *what* we crave. What our souls really hunger for and craves is to know God and to become intimately connected to Him. He can help us break unhealthy eating patterns. God is in the business of changing lives. Turning to Him empowers healing and transformation!

Hidden Addictions

For 20 years I lived conflicted—conflicted between *who I chose to be* and *who God created me to be*. Inevitably, pain and damage in various forms resulted. If we believe we're worthless, unworthy of love, or insignificant, these beliefs will present themselves in our thinking and actions. Our behavior matches our identity. We do destructive things based out of fear instead of love.

The Message paraphrase of Proverbs 21:17 reads, *"You're addicted to thrills? What an empty life! The pursuit of pleasure is never satisfied."*

I've heard mental health experts say obsessive/compulsive behaviors often come in multiples because one addiction often leads to another. Most of us have other "hidden addictions." I juggled at least ten addictions at one time: to food, body image, alcohol, fitness, tanning, collecting vintage dolls and teddy bears; to people-pleasing, perfectionism, even to certain emotions. Each one was a counterfeit means of fulfillment in that I took each thing that was good and distorted it until it became an idol.

We know that an unquenchable desire for food, drugs, alcohol, nicotine, shoplifting, and gambling can destroy lives. However, multitudes of people are hooked on things that don't fit the addiction stereotype: love, work, sports, people-pleasing, perfectionism, cosmetic treatments, shopping, exercising, academics—even pain, control, and chaos. Add to the list: technology, religious activities, watching TV, risk taking, celebrity worship, gaming, tattooing, tanning—even rescuing others, love for pets and children.

These are usually perceived as healthy activities. Yet, each one has the potential to become a fixation or idol. From the brain's perspective, whatever we do to produce feelings of euphoria, is worth repeating. Ultimately, we end up mastered by those things. Ask God to show you if there are other areas of bondage that must be addressed.

Jesus said, *"Here I am! I stand at the door and knock. If anyone hears my voice and opens the door, I will come in and eat with him, and he with me" (Revelation 3:20).* Remember, you're not bound to a religion, but a Person. *He loves you no matter what you've done or how you feel about yourself.*

Healing Essentials

Food and body sculpting activities can become dependencies, unhealthy obsessions. What you may not realize is you have a *codependent relationship* with food or exercise or dieting. Think carefully, have any of these become your god or idol? Has food become your best friend or parent? Does exercise give you a high? Does dieting make you feel sexy?

Whether we realize it or not, deep inside we all feel "something" is missing. Our need to be filled up is God-given because God created us to be overfilled by Him first. We're designed to hold Him as the object of our deepest affections. When we don't, a hole in our soul is exposed. We cannot stand for the hole to be empty so we stuff it with all sorts of things which become the lord of our lives. Yet we're never satisfied because only God can fill us sufficiently.

Many of us also have a daddy hole. The importance of fathers in the lives of daughters has recently received a lot of attention. *Father hunger* is a term that expresses the emptiness experienced by women whose fathers were emotionally absent. That void often leads to distorted body image, yo-yo dieting, food fears, and disordered eating patterns.

There's only one person, one Daddy, who can fill our soul-hole—Jesus Christ. In the Gospels distressed people: the diseased and the wealthy, both men and women, young and old, came to Jesus for healing and counsel. He guided His disciples through emotional and spiritual problems. He even gave life-changing counsel to the repentant thief on the cross. Today He still loves and counsels us through His Word and by His Spirit. Jesus said numerous times, "Follow me." *"I will instruct you and teach you in the way you should go; I will counsel you and watch over you" (Psalm 32:8).* We decide if we want to follow and become active participants in the process.

This Is Your Future

God loves you too much to leave you in your personal food and diet hell. If you *really* want to have victory over unhealthy eating patterns you must first know God, the Father, and His Word in a deeper way. This is the heart of this devotional study; seeing and feeding on the truth, discerning what it means, and applying the truths to your life today.

"This is what the LORD says: I have heard your prayer and seen your tears; I will heal you" (2 Kings 20:5). God offers us hope, and joy flows from hope. Notice God doesn't say when. The process of healing is different for every person and goes by God's timetable, not ours. Growth takes time. It also takes the discipline of prayer, study, heart searching, sensitivity to the Holy Spirit's leading, and consistent compliance.

God may use a variety of vehicles to help you: Bible and/or support groups, a counselor, pastor, or trustworthy friend. But He will always point you to the Bible—His Word—as His vehicle to help you overcome and experience real spiritual transformation.

Are you ready for a God-extreme makeover—to be transformed by Christ and not the culture? Get ready to go to the hardest place, the place where you don't want to go, and meet God there.

As I spent more time with God and incorporated a daily devotional plan into my week, I felt God touch and speak to me, giving me renewed hope.

Prayer and meditation is how we communicate and connect with God. Prayer is speaking to God, a two-way conversation. Meditation is actively listening to Him. Some of God's communications can be both bitter and sweet. The idea is you spend time together. You talk and share thoughts. This is *prayer*. There are no risks in entrusting your thoughts and secrets to God. He already knows them. Many people turn away from their 'object of attachment' as their love and passion for God deepens. Usually the expectation of the person praying is one of receiving back both reward and relationship.

Personal change comes through knowing God and studying the Bible. The Bible is the ongoing story of God's relationship with humanity. It wasn't merely given to us to inform us, but transform and guide us to truth and healing. There's no doubt, the Bible is still relevant for today. *"All Scripture is given by inspiration of God,"* meaning the words are the expression of God's mind, therefore trustworthy (2 Timothy 3:16–17). In other words, *the Bible gives us hope.*

Psalm 19:7 declares, *"The instructions of the LORD* [which come through the Holy Bible] *are perfect, reviving the soul"* (NLT). The psalmist proclaimed, *"I will never forget your commandments, for by them you give me life"* (Psalm 119:93, NLT).

When God sends out His word He heals and rescues His people from the grave (see Psalm 107:20). He revives our dead souls.

No one is changed by an unread Bible. The Bible provides the power to do what needs to be done. It doesn't provide a verse for every single circumstance we face in life. Clearly, we live in a different time and culture than its authors. But the more we live in the context of Scripture as a whole, the more wisdom and discernment we have in daily living. Spend time reading the Bible every day, both the Old and New Testament. Study it. Memorize it. Saturate your thoughts with it. Immerse your soul in it. Drink deeply of its truth. Allow it to run through your veins. Don't look at it as adding one more thing to your already busy schedule. When we make time for God's Word, it has a way of putting all of our activities into perspective.

Journal. This study requires writing out how you feel. One way to begin breaking down our walls is through journaling. Many find it helpful in coming to terms with the past, or processing fresh pain. Feelings and assumptions you didn't even know you had will slip out onto paper as your heart begins to unfold. No one will read what you write except you (so grammar and spelling don't count!). Enter your thoughts and emotions, any physical sensations, and whatever comes to your mind. Journaling is a tool that enhances emotional growth and recovery. It will also become a record of your breakthroughs! Use the "This is How I Feel Chart" in Appendix A to help you answer the questions and exercises in this study, and share with your group (if you are in a group).

Please seek professional help if your feelings begin to overwhelm you.

Solitude is the key. Give yourself adequate time to read, reflect, meditate, and pray alone. Whether you put aside 30 minutes or two hours, being alone with God has a medicinal effect.

Be vigilant! Spiritual growth is not an easy journey. We often find ourselves fleeing back to what's comfortable because we're seeking that "normal" feeling. We'll usually find prayer and Bible study becomes more difficult in these times. Therefore, every day, before you begin reading your Bible and this book, pray. We have an enemy that will use whatever means possible to distract you—such as your own mind, other people, and noise. Ask the Holy Spirit to open your mind and heart to His voice, teaching and direction.

Ask for and accept help. The Israelites fought the Amalekites in Exodus 17. Verse 11 reads, "*As long as Moses held up his hands, the Israelites were winning, but whenever he lowered his hands, the Amalekites were winning."* When Moses tired in battle he sat on a stone. If he remained tired Aaron and Hur each took an arm and held his hands up until the Israelites claimed victory. Each of us needs an Aaron and a Hur—companions who aren't afraid to be with us in the midst of our battles, and strong enough to lift us up when our own strength fails. Each of us needs to be like Moses. A mighty warrior who sat down when he was tired and accepted the help others offered.

Pre-Study Reflective Exercise

Do you want to live free or live a slave in bondage?

Our healing journey begins with the acceptance of our wounded self *and* the desire to let God take control. Matthew 18:1-4 says,

> *"At that time the disciples came to Jesus and asked, "Who is the greatest in the kingdom of heaven?" He called a little child and had him stand among them. And he said: "I tell you the truth, unless you change and become like little children, you will never enter the kingdom of heaven. Therefore, whoever humbles himself like this child is the greatest in the kingdom of heaven."*

Previously, Jesus had been sharing with the disciples the truth about His upcoming suffering and death. Apparently, this forthcoming traumatic event didn't even faze them. In true human form, they were focused on themselves and what position they'd have in His kingdom.

The first thing Jesus said was, *"I tell you the truth."* This is the same man who said, *"The truth will set you free"* (John 8:32). This means anything that is *not* the truth cannot make us free. He continued, *"… unless you change …"* In other words, your current way of living isn't working for you. You're missing the mark. But the knowledge of truth can free us from any fear of change. Then Jesus told them what had to change—they needed to humble themselves. True humility means knowing and accepting ourselves, and knowing and accepting the truth.

I believe Jesus uses a child as an example because children haven't lived in the world long enough to develop negative patterns of behavior. Children typically possess characteristics of humility. He's urging us to return to the simplicity that defines a child: vulnerability, ignorance, innocence, purity, and trust. Children don't know what it means to hate, or hold resentment, or wish animosity on their neighbor, or repay evil with evil. They believe what they hear and love their parents with full affection, despite their shortcomings.

Jesus is talking to us too. We cannot see the face of God unless we become like little children. He's asking us, "Do you want to heal? Are you willing to change? Can you handle the truth? Will you become like a little child?" Open the door to your heart and let God bathe it with the power of truth so the healing process can begin. Restoration is possible *if we do it God's way.* The Bible says, *"Let us examine our ways and test them, and let us return to the Lord" (Lamentations 3:40).*

Before beginning the study take some time to reflect on this passage. Then write the answers to these questions in your journal.

- How is your current way of living working for you? *It's sufficient for now, but I'm afraid I'll regret it in the future*
- What is it you don't want anyone, including God, to know about you? *That I'm not good enough.*
- Finish these sentences, "What presently stands in my way of a free life is … because I …" *me --- do what I do not want, and what I want I do not do*
- "I have insecurities about … that prevent me from feeling and dealing with my issues, and ultimately healing. I think this may be because …" *my status in every aspect of life (compared to others). --- I have made success an idol.*
- If a billboard of your life appeared on a freeway, what would you want it to say? *She is content.*

There is no problem God cannot handle. He has a purpose and a plan if we allow Him to be Lord. He will use everything you learn week-by-week to heal you if you let Him. Be patient. Give God time. You'll experience growth in all areas of your life through an increased sense of self-worth and self-esteem.

"May the God of hope fill you with all joy and peace as you trust in him, so that you may overflow with hope by the power of the Holy Spirit" (Romans 15:13).

Week 1

Pursue Perfection God's Way

God knows.

Maria greeted her family with a smile and tried not to show how much she hurt inside. Today, the doctor told her, once again, to lose weight. She is putting too much stress on her heart and joints. But she loves the comfort rich foods bring. *I know I'm fat. At least my doctor is honest with me. Everybody else just tells me what a pretty face I have.*

By day Kim is an outgoing sales manager on the move. By night she hides in her apartment and goes on uncontrollable feeding frenzies. Kim discovered she could eat everything she wanted and still lose weight with self-induced vomiting and by ingesting laxatives. She's lived with bulimia for fifteen years and swears she'll stop. *Today is the last day.* She cannot beat the cycle.

Anna, a mother of two, loves to cook for her family, but her family barely notices she doesn't eat her own cooking. Anna is determined to stay thin at any cost, which includes restricting her daily diet to 300 calories and abusing substances like diet pills and diuretics. Daily her small frame weakens, yet she wants to be thinner. *If I just lose five more pounds, then I'll be truly happy!*

Jasmine gets up at 3 a.m. to exercise for three hours before school. She feels extremely guilty for missing a workout despite recurring injuries.

Katrina looks in the mirror and sees "repulsive," "fat," "stupid," even though friends tell her she is one of the most intelligent and beautiful girls in her college. *If I'm so beautiful, why can't I see it?*

Perhaps you see yourself in one or all of these women. I did. I did all I could to hide the secrets and my character flaws from friends, family, and God. Yet God knew everything. He knows everything about you too. You may erroneously assume that He feels about you the way you feel about yourself, or that He's allowed you to become addicted. If we hate ourselves, we assume God hates us too. If so, you really don't know Him.

Like any other person, if we do not take the time to get to know our heavenly Father then we'll most likely find we're not able to see ourselves as His child and trust Him for our healing or future. This is why we're going to talk about God's character first. The apostle Peter said,

> *"Do you want more and more of God's kindness and peace? Then learn to know him better and better. For as you know him better, he will give you, through his great power, everything you need for living a truly good life: he even shares his own glory and his own goodness with us!" (2 Peter 1:2–3, TLB)*

Did you get that? Prepare for big changes! Let God be your light and guide. He's a safe Person. God will provide the encouragement and patience to persevere and enable powerful transformation.

Day One: Who Is God?

> *The first thing you must learn, dear friend, is that "the kingdom of God is within you" (Mark 17:21). Never look for the kingdom anywhere but there, within. Once you have realized that the kingdom of God is within you and can be found there, just come to the Lord.* —Madame Jeanne Guyon

What is your current view of God?

When I speak of God I am referring to Him as Father, as Son (Jesus Christ), and Holy Spirit—one God in three Persons. Each one is absolutely equal. They work together. They love and serve. This is God.

Do you know God? If you've never developed a relationship with God, it may be because you were given faulty information about Him when you were a child. Or, perhaps you have a distorted, negative relationship with your earthly father. If your earthly father was demanding, abusive, controlling, or a perfectionist, you may think of God this way.

Perhaps you fear God. You learned He's an angry wrathful judge. Possibly you feel God is distant and impersonal, or has abandoned His created. The truth is God is near. The apostle Paul proclaimed, *"He is not far from each one of us" (Acts 17:27).*

If you don't love yourself then you'll have a hard time believing God could love you. Replacing negative perceptions about God with perceptions that are true is an integral part of understanding God as a power you can trust. Contrary to what you may have been taught, God is *the perfect Father.* He's the picture of compassion and love. Recognize He stands ready to adopt *you* into His family as His cherished daughter. He longs for *your* company.

You may think, *No one seems to care, or notices what is going on with me, so why should God? He's the God of "big things," like miracles.* The Bible says, *"God is love. ... Whoever does not love does not know God, because God is love" (John 4:16; 1 John 4:8).* Pastor and author A. W. Tozer wrote, "True faith requires that we believe everything that God has said about Himself, but also that we believe everything He has said about us!"

Our impressions of God may be very different from the God the Bible actually portrays. He says, "I am love. This is who I am. And I love *you completely.*" As you read the Bible, you'll see it is one big love letter from God. "I love you!" is said over and over.

Each of us was born with an innate desire to be loved unconditionally, but many of us don't feel unconditionally loved and are in pain. Jesus said, *"For God so loved the world* [loved you] *that he gave his one and only Son, that whoever believes in him shall not perish but have eternal life" (John 3:16).* God's love is free for anyone! Lisa Harper wrote,

"The God who spoke the universe into existence, who breathed life into Adam, who stretched out the heavens and the necks of giraffes, has looked down, taken our hand in his, and said, "Yep, she's mine." Even though we're crippled, we have been royally adopted by the King of kings and Lord of lords. We are listed as his next of kin. Our names are written on his hands and in his book of life. His love for us is based on his character, not our performance. And it is greater than we could ever hope for or imagine."[3]

Accept that God loves you right now, exactly the way you are, no matter what you've done. Let His love cover everything in your life. Let Him wrap you with grace and mercy.

I AM

In Exodus 3:13-14 Moses asks God what His name is. God replies, "I AM WHO I AM." We ask, "You are what?" You'll notice as you begin studying the Bible that God often defines Himself by stating, "I am …" Although God is shrouded in mystery, He reveals enough to serve His purpose and for His children to know the truth about Him. God defines Himself by:

Who He Is

"I am compassionate" (Exodus 22:27). "I am merciful" (Jeremiah 3:12). "I am your shield" (Genesis 15:1). "He is kind to the ungrateful and wicked" (Luke 6:35).

What He Feels and Thinks

"I love you with an everlasting love. So I will continue to show you my kindness" (Jeremiah 31:3). "I am the LORD; that is my name! I will not give my glory to another or my praise to idols" (Isaiah 42:8).

What He Chooses to Do

"God is not a man, that he should lie, nor a son of man, that he should change his mind. Does he speak and then not act? Does he promise and not fulfill?" (Numbers 23:19) "This is the confidence we have in approaching God: that if we ask anything according to his will, he hears us" (1 John 5:14). "God will meet all your needs according to his glorious riches in Christ Jesus" (Philippians 4:19). "... comforts us in all our troubles" (2 Corinthians 1:3-4).

He is Faithful

"The Lord is good. He is a fortress in the day of trouble. He knows those who seek shelter in him" (Nahum 1:7). "For the Lord is good and his love endures forever; his faithfulness continues through all generations" (Psalm 100:5).
God is always true to His promises. The psalmist said God never changes (Psalm 102:27). He can never draw back from His promises of blessing or of

judgment. Since He cannot lie, He's unwavering to what He has spoken (Deuteronomy 7:9; 2 Timothy 2:13).

The Real God

Holocaust survivor Corrie ten Boom said, "Never be afraid to trust an unknown future to a known God." Give God a chance to show you who He really is. Never in your life will God express His will toward you except as perfect love. God will never give you second best like man will. St. Augustine said, "God loves each one of us as though there were only one of us to love." It's true!

God is Omniscient [All-Knowing]

Our issues with food have isolated most of us. We live in secrecy, hiding our true feelings and masking our real selves. God knows each secret. He knows everything—past, present, or future (Job 37:16; Psalm 139:1–6). Job 9:4 says God's *"wisdom is profound, his power is vast."* Whenever God expresses Himself to us, we can be confident His directions are accurate.

God is Omnipresent [He is Present Everywhere]

God sees everything. He is near, far, in heaven, and on earth with us (Proverbs 15:3). Jeremiah 23:23–24 says, *"'Am I only a God nearby,' declares the Lord, 'and not a God far away? Can anyone hide in secret places so that I cannot see him?' declares the Lord. 'Do not I fill heaven and earth?'"* God is present everywhere, in the entire universe, at all times. *"Nothing in all creation is hidden from God's sight"* (Hebrews 4:13).

God is Omnipotent [He is All-Powerful]

The scientific community is known for ignoring the greatest source of power in the universe: the power of God. God can bring into being anything He chooses with or without the use of any means. Psalm 147:5 says, *"Great is our Lord and mighty in power; His understanding has no limit."* The same power that raised Christ from the dead can bring you back to life. We must continually remind ourselves that we don't live by the wisdom of men but by the power of God (1 Corinthians 2:5).

God Restores and Renews

1 Corinthians 2:9 states, *"No eye has seen, no ear has heard, no mind has conceived what God has prepared for those who love him."* I've got great news for you! God's prepared to restore us to our real selves and to heal our wounds. This is the same God that said, *"I am making everything new!"* (Revelation 21:5). "New" means fresh; different than before; original. He promises:

- *"I will give you a new heart and put a new spirit in you"* (Ezekiel 36:26).
- *"This means that anyone who belongs to Christ has become a new person. The old life is gone; a new life has begun!"* (2 Corinthians 5:17, NLT).
- *"Your old sin-loving nature was buried with him by baptism when he died; and when God the Father, with glorious power, brought him back to life again, you were given his wonderful new life to enjoy"* (Romans 6:4, TLB).
- *"... put on the new self, which is being renewed in knowledge in the image of its Creator"* (Colossians 3:10).

Day Two: The Great Physician

You have me endure many terrible troubles. You restore me to life again. You bring me back from the depths of the earth. —Psalm 71:20

"Jehovah-Rapha" is the God who heals.

The God who healed the woman with a food addiction or the one abused by her father is the same God who can heal *you*. More than two thousand years ago, Plato wrote, "If the head and body are to be well, you must begin with the soul; that is the first thing."

Today science and medicine are recognizing Plato's wisdom by treating addiction with spiritual healing. Our best medical people are following Louis Pasteur's words, "A little science estranges men from God; much science leads them back to him." Medicine owes its greatest debt to Jesus of Nazareth—the great Physician. Time by itself is not a healer. Jesus Christ has the answer for a bruised soul (and body)

In the Old Testament, God was a real holy presence. He summoned His people, Israel, from outside their world. He entered time and space and revealed part of His character to them—to the extent that He chose to, and to the extent that was best for them.

The Israelites were to learn an important principle. God said, *"If you listen carefully to the voice of the Lord your God and do what is right in his eyes, if you pay attention to his commands and keep all his decrees, I will not bring on you any of the diseases I brought on the Egyptians, for I am the Lord, who heals you" (Exodus 15:22–26).*

If the Israelites turned back to God, He would heal them. Many of us have tried program after program and read multitudes of self-help books. Nothing worked. Jeremiah 6:14 says, *"They dress the wound of my people as though it were not serious."* This means we try to heal superficially. These things don't touch our hearts and spirits, or change the inside.

God is the healer of the brokenhearted, *"He is the one who bandages their wounds" (Psalm 147:3).* If we do what God desires, we too can be healed. When things are difficult, run to God. Come to God as one who has no strength of her own. Humbly lay your bruised condition before Him.

Our Wonderful Counselor—the Holy Spirit

We're all looking for direction out of the hole we've gotten ourselves into. Jesus said the Holy Spirit, our Counselor, would guide us into all truth (John 16:3). There are many misconceptions about the identity of the Holy Spirit.

The Holy Spirit is God, the third Person of the Trinity. This fact is clear in many Scriptures[4] As God, the Holy Spirit can truly function as the Comforter and Counselor that Jesus promised He would be (John 14:16, 26, 15:26).

Think about it this way: when a country is taken over by a new power radical changes follow—revamping, renaming, redirecting, and replacing. So it is with the Holy Spirit. He is inducting His people into a new way of life. We become citizens of a new country—God's country, and the Holy Spirit helps us transition gracefully.

The Holy Spirit will never lead us in the wrong direction like mankind will. He will make our paths straight if we trust Him instead of our own intuition (Proverbs 3:5–6). His concern is not only with the cleansing of past sins and wounds, but our present and future growth into the likeness of Jesus Christ.

Day Three: Face Reality

Who is the greatest in the kingdom of heaven?
> —the disciples, speaking in Matthew 18:1

I'd give anything to be a super-model!

I, like so many other teens, learned quickly that the way to be accepted was through the sculpting of my body—despite the fact the boys in my sixth-grade class told me I could only be a model for *Mad Magazine*. I created collages of j u n i o r models because they represented "perfection" to me. Soon they became my idols. *If I'm a model, then my life will be gratifying!*

An *idol* is anything, or anyone, we put our trust in in order to meet our needs apart from God—a *God substitute*. If we're feeling victimized, the idol may even be our problem. Isaiah 44:17–18 says,

> *"From the rest he makes a god, his idol; he bows down to it and worships. He prays to it and says, 'Save me; you are my god.' They know nothing, they understand nothing; their eyes are plastered over so they cannot see, and their minds closed so they cannot understand."*

Inevitably, my idols made me feel worthless and humiliated because I couldn't measure up to their standards. Since we cannot attain that perfection, we don't feel good about ourselves because our self-esteem is related to our body and self-image. We ignore our genetic code. When we don't feel good about ourselves, it's hard to develop meaningful relationships with God and others.

It's been said that the average woman will spend nearly one year of her life trying to decide what to wear. Whatever happened to the importance of inner beauty? The Bible says, *"The Lord does not look at the things man looks at. Man looks at the outward appearance, but the Lord looks at the heart"* (1 Samuel 16:7). This is where authentic beauty resides. Real beauty isn't found in seeking to be praised or great. It's in the heart.

What is the state of your heart today? We cannot spend day after day in this world without it affecting our minds, our hearts, and our souls. They become unguarded. Our hearts start to shift away from God. And the ironic thing is the harder we work to become free, the more freedom we seem to lose. It is no surprise King Solomon advised, *"**Above all else,** guard your heart [or affections] for it is the wellspring of life"* (Proverbs 4:23, my emphasis).

The Truth about Bondage

One big reason we're enslaved to our appearances is because our hearts become unguarded and we're manipulated by the lies the media feeds us. Our hearts believe physical beauty will bring satisfaction and recognition. False promises like, *If I'm beautiful ... then I'll be happy and successful. I'll be popular and desirable to men. I'll know lasting intimacy and true love. I'll be secure, important, significant, and confident.*

There are other factors that contribute to a flawed view of ourselves and abnormal eating habits. One factor is a dysfunctional family system in which there is a lot of control and dependency, or performance pressure in the area of grades, or other parent appointed activities. Depression may be a factor. Or involvement in sports that promote thinness or appearance-oriented activities.

Our attitudes toward our bodies and appearance influence our eating patterns. What were you told about your body and food when you were a child? How often were you complimented about your appearance? Were you teased or prodded to lose weight relentlessly?

God knows women want to look attractive. The Bible even speaks about many beautiful women. Yet Scripture tells us to, *"Cultivate inner beauty, the gentle, gracious kind that God delights in"* (1 Peter 3:3–5, MSG). There is beauty in integrity, intelligence, humor, simplicity, and complexity. Can you think of other examples?

Where Do You Fall on the Perfection Scale?

No one can do the superwoman dance every day before her dance shoes give out. If there is a single quality which characterizes perfect people it's a powerful, unconscious need to feel in control. It often starts by attempting to master or restrain our self, but can quickly develop into a desire to dominate and influence others.

Circle or underline each statement that describes you:

- The more beautiful and thin I am, the happier I'll be.
- My appearance will help me achieve my goals and dreams.
- I am fat and ashamed of my appearance.
- I won't be happy until I fix some of my physical characteristics.
- If I eat anything that contains sugar or fat, I'll get fat.
- If I don't have the "right" look, then I won't have the best job, relationships, and, ultimately, happiness.
- I am not a very attractive person.

If you believe any one of these statements, you are a perfectionist. They each represent a lie, or wrong assumption, and lead to negative self-image.

Everyone has beauty but not everyone sees it. It doesn't depend on what our peers say or what our culture currently reflects. True self-worth and beauty, true perfection, is seeing ourselves as God sees us. Let's begin to look up to someone real—God, and take our focus off worldly images and messages. God has already made promises to you. As you study, He'll begin to give you a picture of who you really are.

Day Four: God's Perfection

When a child of God looks into the Word of God, she sees the Son of God and is changed by the Spirit of God into the image of God for the glory of God.

–Unknown

Physical beauty does not ensure happiness.

Agnes Repplier said, "It's not easy to find happiness in ourselves and it is not possible to find it elsewhere." Throughout history, the lives of some of the most physically attractive women have often been tragic and pitiful. In this culture, image is everything. But the image that really counts is found elsewhere.

Twenty-seven verses into the Bible we're given a declaration about life. *We are images of a greater being.* The focus is on something *in us.* Genesis 1:27 says, *"God created man in his own image, in the image of God he created him; male and female he created them."* Image of God simply means "made like God."

After studying God's character earlier this week, does your image of God bear any resemblance to your own self-image? No? That's because most of us have a negative self-image because the focus has been on things *outside of us*. A. W. Tozer wrote,

> "The whole purpose of God in redemption is to make us holy and to restore us to the image of God. To accomplish this, He disengages us from earthly ambitions and draws us away from the cheap and unworthy prizes that worldly men set their hearts upon."

Are you ready to nurture a new image of a new you?

The Power of Love

In the Bible, there are frequent passages about God's unconditional love and people's sins. Israel turned her back to God numerous times. You'd think that God would throw His hands up and say, "I give up on you! You can no longer be my people." Yet He doesn't. Time after time, Jesus's disciples disappointed Him. At the moment of crisis, they deserted Him. However, He never stopped loving them—because God *is* love.

We are born with an innate God-given need to be loved. The first people that must love us are our parents. If we don't receive their love, deep down we'll feel something isn't right. Psychologists call this "love hunger" and refer to our need for love as a deep need to fill our *love tank*.

Love tanks help us understand our basic love needs. When our love tanks aren't filled, life tends to be a struggle. If your love tank is on low or empty, let God fill it. Our tanks fill up and we function better when we worship and serve Him. God wants to be loved by you![5]

Be Perfect, As Your Heavenly Father Is Perfect

If you're like me, you know what it feels like to *need* to please everyone and gain their approval. *I must create the perfect body and land the perfect man and job so I'll be admired and loved.* Maybe you thought if you ever did anything wrong that you wouldn't be liked by your parents, friends, or teachers. Maybe you think if you're not perfect, you won't be loved or accepted.

Having extreme rules and standards by which we measure ourselves leads to self-criticism and personal torment. The day came when I admitted I wasn't perfect and could never be perfect. I knew I needed God. This was good! But then I read the verse, *"Be perfect, therefore, as your heavenly Father is perfect" (Matthew 5:48)*. Huh?

The word "perfect" is the Greek word *teleios*, and is translated to mean "mature, fully developed." It doesn't refer to flawless or moral perfection, but to the kind of love that is like God's love—mature, complete, openhearted to all, and full of blessing. "You must be perfect," means we are to, one, seek to love others as wholeheartedly as God loves us; and two, fulfill the purpose for which we were made.

Perhaps you said to a loved one, "You want me to succeed, but what if I failed? Could you still love me?" No matter what we've done or what we'll do, we are a success. This is because God has already set into motion an amazing plan for our lives. *"Many are the plans in a man's heart, but it's the LORD's purpose that prevails" (Proverbs 19:21)*. There are those who will love us whether we fail or succeed.

Oswald Chambers said, "As soon as God becomes real, other people become shadows. Nothing that other saints do or say can ever perturb the one who is built on God."[6]

If you do something ninety-nine percent perfect but still feel you're defective because of the one percent imperfection recognize that Christ died for you because you can never be perfect. He died so *you don't have to be perfect!*

Day Five: Break the Cover Girl Mask

The perpetual delusion of humanity is thinking we are better off hiding than confessing, avoiding rather than facing, clinging to our sickness instead of taking the remedy that's freely given and readily available. –Mark Buchanan

Masks are interesting phenomena.

One reason we create a mask is to conceal our perceived identities and cover-up our lives. Another reason is we feel we have nothing secure to fall back on. Genesis 3 gives us an explanation. After disobeying God and eating the fruit Genesis 3:8-10 states,

Then the man and his wife heard the sound of the LORD God as he was walking in the garden in the cool of the day, and they hid from the LORD God among the trees of the garden.

But the LORD God called to the man, "Where are you?"

He answered, "I heard you in the garden, and I was afraid because I was naked; so I hid."

This passage implies God was with them in human form (like Christ on earth was). Sin did not separate God and mankind. He walked with them in direct fellowship. God called to the man, Adam, "Where are you?" Why would God ask this when nothing in all creation is hidden from God's sight? He was giving him an opportunity to come forth and admit his sin— to confess.

Adam says, *I heard ya. I didn't want you to see me naked! So I hid.* In other words, *I'm feeling fearful and shameful.* Not surprising, when we lose our security, fear sets in and we lose our hearts. We hide because we feel ashamed and guilty. This is silly because we can't hide from God.

After each binge purge episode … each one night stand … each drunken incident, I felt naked and ashamed … and I hid. Then I'd pull myself together and put on my carefully crafted Cover Girl mask and face the day.

Denial = Don't Even Notice I Am Lying

Denial is all the things we tell ourselves to rationalize, justify, or minimize our unhealthy patterns. *Everybody struggles with weight, body image, and food issues. I'm just like everyone else.* Denial is a mask and a common emotional reaction when we're confronted with our obsessions about food or our bodies.

Convincing ourselves that our lives are working successfully is a form of denial. It's a self-protecting behavior that keeps us from honestly facing the truth. Jesus said, *"Why do you look at the speck of sawdust in your brother's eye and pay no attention to the plank in your own eye?" (Luke 6:41).*

Denial is a powerful tool the enemy uses. Never underestimate its ability to cloud your vision. Before we can truly grow in our faith and experience God's healing, we must first face and admit our denial.

Admit to God you've been abusing yourself and endangering your health through compulsive exercise, fad dieting, starvation, bingeing and purging, overeating, laxative and substance abuse, isolation, or codependency. He already knows but is waiting for you to recognize your dependencies. If you've done this then you've just broken through a concrete wall of denial *and* broken the power the devil had over you!

The Mask of Pride

Psychologist Gregory Jantz, author of *Hope, Help, and Healing for Eating Disorders* wrote,

> "One of the prime factors in denial is that of pride. Pride encourages the denial of your eating disorder. If you are anorexic, you've got denial down pat—and you take an enormous amount of pride in the accomplishment of your weight loss. If you overeat, you may tell yourself your behavior is normal due to your difficult circumstances—*I just need to feel better; and then I'll stop.* If you are a compulsive overeater, you are probably past the point of pretending that what you do is normal, but your pride may be keeping you from crying out for help."[7]

Today's the last day! If you binge or are bulimic, you probably believe you have enough willpower (self-power) to quit. I did.

Some say we are all born with a mask of pride and selfishness. My mask of pride morphed into a monster mask, and it wasn't discarded after Halloween. It was a spiritual virus that infected my life. I learned the pride I developed as a child had a motivating effect on the development of my abnormal eating patterns.

Pride is blinding. As my eating patterns changed for the worst, pride whispered that my behavior was acceptable. This kept me from seeking help. Pride took center stage. *Look at what I've accomplished! I'm in control. Look, I'm a size 4!* In everything I did, I made certain that I got the credit. This was false self-confidence.

Pride is deceptive. We aspire to be number one because of self-importance and the need to be accepted. Instead of working toward our personal best (a *spirit of excellence*), we are determined to be better than everyone else (*spirit of perfection*). Proverbs 27:2 says not to praise ourselves, but let others do it . . . if they only would!

Have you read the book of Obadiah? Have you heard of the book of Obadiah? It is a message to the country of Edom in Israel. Obadiah 1:1–4 has a message to us all:

> *"This is what the Sovereign Lord says about Edom—We have heard a message from the Lord: An envoy was sent to the nations to say, "Rise, and let us go against her for battle"—"See, I will make you small among the nations; you will be utterly despised. The pride of your heart has deceived you, you who live in the clefts of the rocks and make your home on the heights, you who say to yourself, 'Who can bring me down to the ground?' Though you soar like the eagle and make your nest among the stars, from there I will bring you down," declares the Lord."*

Maybe you've earned that promotion, dropped down a dress size, got the coolest car, or surgically changed a feature. You may think you're soaring through life, feeling you have control over everything—you feel good enough to touch the stars. Obadiah reminds us that *we are not in control—* God is in control. And let us also not forget, *"Every good and perfect gift is from above, coming down from the Father of the heavenly lights, who does not change like shifting shadows"* (James 1:17).

The Mask of Jealousy and Envy

In high school, I became friends with a cheerleader. Not only was she beautiful, smart, popular, and dated the captain of the football team, but she was wealthy and drove a sports car. *I'd give anything to be her! Why don't glamorous things happen to me?*

For decades, *Jealous* was my name. This green-eyed ugly monster reared its horrid head predominately in every intimate relationship, consuming my life on many levels. Jealousy seems to come so naturally. But unchecked it results in envy, criticism, resentment, and gossip. Rooted in the soil of low self-esteem, it grows branches of comparison and noxious thorns of desire for what others have.

This emotion has been around for a long time. In the first book of the Bible, Cain murdered Abel because of it (Genesis 4:8). God knew envy was so soul-destroying that He prohibited it in the Ten Commandments.

James 4:1-2 states,

"What causes fights and quarrels among you? Don't they come from your desires that battle within you? You want something but don't get it. You kill and covet, but you cannot have what you want. You quarrel and fight. You do not have, because you do not ask God."

The answer to managing the stress of these emotions is to *ask God.* Eventually I realized I'd compared the *inside of me* to the *outside of her.* I looked at her in her evening gown whilst standing there in my underwear. I found if I took the time and examined her, her "inside" was just as disorderly, or more so. Then I was grateful for the blessings God had bestowed upon me. By the way—that beautiful, wealthy, popular cheerleader struggled with alcoholism and married four times.

How then do we remedy Exodus 20:5: *"You must not bow down to them or worship them* [idols], *for I, the LORD your God, am a jealous God who will not tolerate your affection for any other gods"* (NLT). Scripture can help us answer Scripture. Joshua told the people, *"You will not be able to serve the LORD, for He is a holy God. He is a jealous God" (Joshua 24:19-20, NASB).*

God's jealousy is holy jealousy which is rooted in unconditional, godly love. Man's jealousy is toxic because it's rooted in expectations and misguided conditional love. I've heard it said, "He that is not jealous is not in love." The *King James Version* of Deuteronomy 4:24 says *"the LORD thy God is a consuming fire, even a jealous God."* This sounds like a deep, passionate love to me!

God longs for an intimate and eternal relationship with us and He's not ashamed to admit it. His jealousy springs out of His concern He may lose us to some other god such as another person, or money, or to an obsession with our appearance, or to substances and activities.

"Emotional" jealousy is Satan's lie. It's toxic and wreaks havoc in our lives because we focus on earthly people and things, not on God. Toxic jealousy hurts our relationship with others, and more so our relationship with God. Proverbs 14:30 says, *"A heart at peace gives life to the body, but envy rots the bones."* Envy is spiritual osteoporosis!

Remember, someone will always be prettier or smarter or thinner. Her house will be bigger. She'll drive a better car. Her children will do better in school. Her husband will be more successful. Let it go—love yourself and your circumstances.

God says, *"Charm and grace are deceptive, and beauty is vain [because it is not lasting], but a woman who worshipfully reveres the Lord, she shall be praised!"* (Proverbs 31:30, AMP). When you begin to feel God's constant love and care, toxic jealousy will be interrupted and replaced with holy jealousy and love.

The Mask of Judgment

"Looking back, I realize just how much of my life has been spent dwelling upon the faults of others. It provided self-satisfaction, but I see now just how subtle and actually perverse the process became. After all was said and done, the net effect of judging others was self-granted permission to remain comfortably unaware of my own defects." –Lana

Romans 2:1 forces us to look into the mirror, *"for at whatever point you judge the other, you are condemning yourself, because you who pass judgment do the same things."*

Do you thrive on judging the faults of others? I did all the time, and why not? I believed, *Others judge me, and God judges us!* Again, how do we remedy that God judges others? The answer is the same. God's character is perfectly moral. He rules with holy divine judgment. Psalm 7:11 states, *"God is a righteous judge."* We're not. Our actions are rooted solely in our emotions. In our insecurity, we unconsciously believe that if we can find faults in others, then we'll feel better about ourselves.

As a part of His sovereignty and authority, God is the only one who has the authority to judge the created order. Let God be judge. He's given us more important things to work on.

When it comes to each mask, Paul gives us some great advice,

"Whatever is true, whatever is noble, whatever is right, whatever is pure, whatever is lovely, whatever is admirable—if anything is excellent or praiseworthy—think about such things" (Philippians 4:8).

The Message paraphrase reads, *"I'd say you'll do best by filling your minds and meditating on things true, noble, reputable, authentic, compelling, gracious—the best, not the worst; the beautiful, not the ugly; things to praise, not things to curse."*

In other words, think about the constructive—not destructive. Notice the first thing he says to think on is *truth*. We must evaluate what is going on in our minds and ask, "Does truth occupy the high ground in my mind?" If not, then we can expect negative consequences to happen (which come out of wrong or corrupt beliefs). The one person we should compare ourselves to is Jesus. We ask ourselves, "Will I ever have to deny what I'm about to do?" and "What would Jesus think and do in this situation?"

Through the power of the Holy Spirit we can learn how to address errors in our thinking and replace them with truth. The key is empowering the Holy Spirit with the spiritual discipline of studying the truth. This means everyday ingesting the Word of God, going to His chat room, and spending time with Him.

Closing Moments

It's not about the masks. It's about becoming vulnerable.

Part of valuing ourselves is taking the necessary steps toward healing and repairing what is broken. It's about letting go of what doesn't work and accepting that we're not and will never be perfect. Masks are created when we try to be perfect and cover up our insecurities. Perfection gets in the way of restoration because it imposes impossible, unrealistic goals that set us up for failure.

When we take our masks off and reveal our true selves, and accept there are dark and dysfunctional parts, then we can begin to fully accept ourselves and find the courage to change. We can claim our identity as God's child and experience pure pleasure in who we are. Then the healing and transforming work truly begins.

We all make mistakes. This is why pencils have erasers! If we don't think we must be perfect, then we can accept our mistakes as learning experiences and be willing to try again.

Good news! God will use our strengths and weaknesses for His glory. Say out loud: *I'm thankful that I don't need to be perfect!* Recall God called

Himself, "I AM WHO I AM." As His daughter, you can say, *I am who I am and I don't need man's approval!*

Promise to Claim: May the words of my mouth and the meditation of my heart be pleasing in your sight, O LORD, my Rock and my Redeemer. (Psalm 19:14)

Week 2

Why Do I Hurt?

Life is pain. The sharper, the more evidence of life.

A few days before my thirty-first birthday, I abruptly lost the vision in my left eye. The diagnosis: optical neuritis. The ophthalmologist indicated I might even lose the sight in my right eye. *Blind! Impossible!* I couldn't imagine what life would be like disabled.

Anguished, I waited days, and then weeks, for dozens of test results to come in. *I must have done this to myself. If only I wasn't bulimic ... if only I could start all over ...* the torment dragged on. Deeply depressed, I bargained with God, *If you make everything better I'll be good. I'll stop bingeing and purging.*

Professionals are convinced, due to pressure I put on my optic nerves when I purged, the eye didn't receive an adequate supply of blood and/or it suffered a stroke. Eventually part of my sight was restored. Today I'm legally blind in that eye. There are always consequences to self-destructive behavior. And I didn't hold up my end of the bargain. I continued to binge and purge because of the grip of addiction, and God wasn't the foundation of my life.

I believe God allows consequences because they serve as instruction. My physical vision may be lacking, but the good news is my spiritual vision gets clearer each day. It's less clouded by self-serving desires and goals. I work to keep my spiritual eyes fixed on God. As we turn our eyes to God in times of pain and struggle, we experience His comfort and hope. He helps us to see more clearly each day.

Suffering isn't pleasant but it's necessary. Pain broadens our base of experience and can make us stronger. Paul taught that suffering is an essential course in God's curriculum (Acts 14:22). We become less judgmental, self-righteous, and less convinced our way is right if we allow ourselves to express and feel pain. We become more compassionate in the end. As we continue to put our hope and trust in God, we'll grow stronger *in spite of* our painful experiences.

Day One: Abducted

You face your greatest opposition when you're closest to your biggest miracle.
—Bishop T. D. Jakes

We live in depressing times.

In a condemning voice, I tell myself, "You're disciplined and smart. Stop it!" Blind to reality I answer myself, "I cannot. The captor gives me acceptance, pleasure, and relief. It demands my loyalty, devotion, and service. It won't release me."

You may remember the story of 11-year-old Jaycee Lee Dugard who was kidnapped in 1991. Abducted from a school bus stop, she went missing for over eighteen years. During this time, Jaycee had two daughters by her abductor. Most people wonder why she simply didn't run away when she had the opportunity. Psychologists have a term to explain this phenomenon: the *Stockholm syndrome.*

Stockholm syndrome is a psychological response that occasionally occurs in people who've been abducted and held hostage. The abductee doesn't resist and actually shows signs of loyalty or caring for the person who took them. They do so despite the dangerous and harmful things the abductor does to them. Instead of hating the abductor, the person befriends and, at times, actually believes the captor is protecting them instead of harming and dominating them. Some people believe this may have happened to Jaycee.

We can use this term, Stockholm syndrome, to understand how a person becomes abducted by addiction. Using an eating disorder as the example, the disorder takes hold of the person's mind and won't let go despite the fact the eating disorder is harmful, even potentially lethal. The abductor (eating disorder) makes the person do many things: starve, binge, purge, take laxatives, or exercise until exhaustion. In return, the abductor offers her a false sense of protection.

The woman held captive believes she controls the power of the eating disorder because she chose it. As a result, she befriends the eating disorder and creates an identity around it. She'll even defend it when other people show concern or try to medically treat her; similar to the abused woman who defends her abuser. Over time she actually believes the eating disorder is helping, not hurting her. It gives the message, "If you're thin, all your problems will disappear. I'm your savior!" It promises life, but ultimately robs you of your very soul.

There's a good chance that right now you feel stressed. You promised yourself you wouldn't engage in a negative or self-destructive behavior. But somehow the abductor baited you with those familiar promises. The liar it is, it starts the process of churning out negative self-talk. You find yourself doing what you don't want to do.

Sin deceives. It whispers, "The abductor will give you what you want. It will take care of you. God won't. He's angry at you." The abductor promises to relieve your pain and fill your soul-hole. Christians have a name for this captor, Satan—and his goal is to silently seduce us, infect our minds, and destroy our lives.

Someone said humans have a tendency to crucify ourselves between two thieves: the regret of yesterday and the fear of tomorrow. The good news is healing and transformation often occur smack in the middle of life's adversities. God knows the lessons we must learn—lessons of patience, submission, and self-denial. When we vent our heart to the Lord, He uses our pain to draw us closer to Him.

Quite often our prayers aren't answered immediately. The Bible tells us not to lose heart (Luke 18:1). Keep praying—don't cease. Sometimes God fulfills our desires. Sometimes He asks us to wait. Sometimes He says no so He can give us something better.

Day Two: Why Must I Suffer?

When life is good we tend to have no questions, but when life is bad we have no answers. –Mike Mason

When we feel imprisoned, we ask, "Where is God?"

One night, Carol was purging for the third time in one hour. All of a sudden, she felt a piercing, stinging sensation in her throat and she began gagging. In the toilet bowl she saw a puddle of blood. *It's okay,* she thought, *I've bled before* (denial). The blood kept coming. *What am I going to do? Who can I tell? Nobody knows my horrible, shameful secret.* The fear became overwhelming. But she still didn't tell anyone.

For the next two days, Carol suffered and existed in agony. On the third day, she checked into the emergency room. She had a very large ulcer in her throat that was on the verge of rupturing, which could lead to death. This is a picture of both physical and emotional suffering. We each have our own stories.

Why does this all-powerful God allow us to suffer so, especially if He is a loving God? The Bible doesn't spell out His reasons, *"How impossible it's for us to understand his decisions and his methods!" (Romans 11:33, TLB).* But the Bible does give us insights into how God uses our difficulties for good.

Peter goes so far as to insist that suffering is our calling. *"To this you were called, because Christ suffered for you, leaving you an example, that you should follow in his steps" (1 Peter 2:22).* Oliver Wendell Holmes understood this truth when he wrote, "If I had a formula for ridding mankind of trouble, I think I would not reveal it, for in doing so, I would do him a disservice."[8]

God has a specific objective in mind. He knows exactly the intensity and duration needed to fulfill His purposes. Through the whole process, whether it's days, weeks, months, or years, we have His promise,

> *"When you pass through the waters, I will be with you; and when you pass through the rivers, they will not sweep over you. When you walk through the fire, you will not be burned; the flames will not set you ablaze" (Isaiah 43:2).*

Every pain in life can take many shapes and forms. God will be with us in those pains, those waters. Scripture doesn't say we won't have bad days. It doesn't tell us that rivers won't roar at our feet. It does however promise *the rivers won't overwhelm us.* Because of God's great love, *we'll not be consumed in the fire.* 1 Peter 5:10 says,

> *"The God of all grace, who called you to His eternal glory in Christ, after you have suffered a little while, will himself restore you and make you strong, firm and steadfast."*

Healed by a Touch

When life is confusing and tumultuous, when fears, shame, and guilt run rampant; when circumstances and people threaten us, we want relief. We want access to the merciful Physician. Mark 5:25–43 speaks of a mystery woman in the crowd who had been slowly bleeding for 12 years. No doubt anemic, she'd suffered a great deal and spent all her money on doctors. Nothing had worked. She was desperate . . . but then heard Jesus was coming. She had hope!

As the crowd gathered, she thought, *If I just touch his clothes, I will be healed.* Notice she goes to Jesus; she doesn't wait around for Him to find her. Jesus got closer. She touched His robe. "Immediately her bleeding stopped and she felt in her body that she was freed from her suffering." Then Jesus asked, "Who touched me?" The woman stepped up. Trembling, she knelt before Him and told her story. No one listened before. But when this woman reached out to Jesus, He said, "Daughter, your faith has healed you. Go in peace and be freed from your suffering." This spells H-O-P-E!

Jewish law considered her unclean, unsocial—a social leper. No one would go near her. Can you imagine the shame? To be shunned by society around-the-clock. Then Jesus called her "daughter." This is the only time in Scripture when He calls a woman "daughter." No longer a mysterious, unnamed woman, Jesus gave her a name when no one else did—a name worthy of a child created in the image of God.

In *Saving Milly* by Morton Kondrake, Michael J. Fox said, "One's dignity may be assaulted, vandalized and cruelly mocked, but cannot be taken away unless it is surrendered." This precious woman became a daughter of the King! After her encounter with Jesus, I'm certain feelings of shame, inferiority, and low self-esteem decreased.

When Jesus walked this planet, He gave dignity and worth to every person. *1 Peter 3:7 says, "... in the new life of God's grace, you're equals" (MSG).* The hand that touched this woman can touch you because Scripture says, *"Jesus Christ is the same yesterday and today and forever" (Hebrews 13:8).*

One woman told me, "The messages I got from my family were always negative. I never felt love or acceptance. Then I touched Jesus and realized God loves me just the way I am!"

The way Jesus related to women was remarkable. In those days, Jewish culture segregated men from women. *Talk not with womankind!* Rabbis would normally avoid speaking to women. None of this was scriptural. It was born out of man's law, not God's.

The way Jesus acted towards women was revolutionary and shocking. Relaxed and open with women, Jesus allowed them to touch and kiss Him, a rabbi. Accepting, sensitive, and affirming, He treated all women with the deepest respect. He is the kind of man God wants every woman to know in her life. You can trust Jesus with your heart.

Day Three: Silver and Gold

The gem cannot be polished without friction, nor man perfected without trials.
–Chinese Proverb

Suffering and glory go together.

God equates our suffering to the purifying of silver and gold. Neither metal is pure in its natural state. Both are mixed with all sorts of gunk making them impure, just like us. Malachi 3:3 says, *"He [God] will sit as a refiner and purifier of silver; he will purify the Levites and refine them like gold and silver."*

Silver and gold must be refined before their beauty is revealed. So do we. We are born with a sinful nature (a result of the Fall) and are influenced by a society permeated with sin. We constantly attract all sorts of impurities: thoughts, beliefs, destructive actions, and habits. The process of refining includes the melting down of the metal by fires designed not to destroy the metal, but bring forth its beauty.

The silver is crushed into small pieces and placed into a crucible. The silversmith places the crucible over the fire and then watches carefully as the silver melts. Eventually, impurities rise to the top. The silversmith scrapes them off carefully. Then a hotter fire is built. Again, the silver is subjected to more heat. Under intense firing, more impurities are released.

The silversmith never leaves the silver unattended in the fire because too much heat may damage the metal. Each time the fire is amplified and impurities removed, the silversmith looks at himself in the melted silver. At first, his image is dim. However, with each new fire his image becomes clearer. When he visibly sees himself, he knows all the impurities are gone. The refining is complete.

God breaks us and puts us into the crucible of suffering for one purpose—to make us into His image. At first, large chunks of impurities surface, representing "big" sins, like stealing and lying. It's somewhat easy to skim these off. The process continues, and with each layer of impurities, the chunks get smaller and smaller. It takes longer to skim off the smaller impurities—representing unidentified sin and negative core beliefs, because they're harder to see.

If you're feeling the heat of the fire today, remember God has His eye on you. He'll keep you close until He sees His image in you and every tiny impurity is removed. Remember, He is *not* the source of your pain. 1 Peter 1:6–7 says,

> *"In this you greatly rejoice, though now for a little while you may have had to suffer grief in all kinds of trials. These have come so that your faith—of greater worth than gold, which perishes even though refined by fire—may be proved genuine and may result in praise, glory and honor when Jesus Christ is revealed."*

Pain—the loss of a dream or an old identity or a valued friend or a childhood—each loss needs space to be acknowledged. Don't be afraid. God is here. He's been there through every trial, pain, and hurt. He's had His hand on each situation so it wouldn't destroy you, knowing that eventually it would work together for good.

If we bypass this part of the journey, we miss more than we realize. God uses situations and tests in our lives to rid us of impurities and teach us that our strength is in Him alone. *To avoid the trials forces us to reject the lessons God wants to teach us.* Learn to see every trial, past, present, and future, as part of God's refining process to make you more like Jesus.

Day Four: Divine Pruning

> *Though he slay me, yet will I trust in him. If he wounds it's to heal . . . He would not thus prune the tree if he had sentenced it to be cut down.* –William Jay

A beautiful, healthy garden requires pruning.

What if I told you that you needed to endure a long, intense, and difficult trial so God could prune away some of the rough edges and sin in your life—a trial that leads to a healthier you. The dictionary says "to prune" is to cut off or remove dead or living parts or branches to improve shape or growth; to remove what is unnecessary or undesirable. Jesus explains:

> *"I am the true vine, and my Father is the gardener. He cuts off every branch in me that bears no fruit, while every branch that does bear fruit he prunes so that it will be even more fruitful. You are already clean because of the word I have spoken to you. Remain in me, and I will remain in you. No branch can bear fruit by itself; it must remain in the vine. Neither can you bear fruit unless you remain in me. I am the vine; you are the branches. If a man remains in me and I in him, he will bear much fruit; apart from me you can do nothing" (John 15:1–5).*

We've all felt pruned. Perhaps it was when your father left home and divorced your mother, or when your boyfriend abandoned you for another woman, or you were passed over for that job or promotion. Pruning is painful but profitable. We need God's help even to desire to yield ourselves to His pruning. Yet His trials are occasions for joy because they test our faith and develop in us perseverance and maturity (character).

"I am the vine; you are the branches. If a man remains in me and I in him, he will bear much fruit; apart from me you can do nothing." What a beautiful description of our personal relationship with Christ. We abide in Him and He in us. We are part of Him, rooted and grounded in Him—as one.

Character Development

A blameless and upright man named Job (the book of Job) is a man who loses everything—all his children, his material wealth, and his health. Yet he proclaimed,

> *"Naked I came from my mother's womb, and naked I will depart. The LORD gave and the LORD has taken away; may the name of the LORD be praised" (Job 1:21).*

The facts don't add up. Job did nothing to deserve these calamities. After reading Job's story, a most common question asked is "Why do the righteous suffer?" The answer: God develops our character through suffering.

Throughout this nightmare, Job moved through a range of emotions, much like we would. He grieved. He got depressed. He wished he was dead. Job gets angry, which is normal because anger accompanies grief. He even painted God as a villain,

> *"God assails me and tears me in his anger and gnashes his teeth at me. Though I cry, 'I've been wronged!' I get no response; though I call for help, there is no justice"* (Job 16:9; 19:7).

These are feelings of entrapment and angst. Job was a tormented man. We can understand why he was bitter, what awful memories he carried in his mind each day. What we don't usually realize is our feelings sometimes lie. Like Job, many people believe their feelings without proving them.

We must place our confidence on God's promises, His Word, and not in our feelings. Our feelings are manipulated by circumstances, other people, hormones, and past experiences. Whereas, God is a promise keeper. We can cling to His promises. They'll never fail. His Word is 100 percent reliable

Had God really abandoned Job? No. Job poses a great number of questions to God, questions he never received answers to. As soon as God spoke to Job, he recognized he shouldn't have challenged God's wisdom. *"I know that you can do all things; no plan of yours can be thwarted"* (Job 42:2). Job's perception of the situation changed. He beheld God's profound greatness in his circumstances.

The theme in the book of Job is one of suffering. But the real story is about faith and the role that suffering plays on faith. The actual plan that falls apart is not God's; it's Satan's.

Throughout the fiery trial, Job's wife survives and eventually bears ten more children. God lifts Job up, blesses him, and restores everything twofold because that's God's nature: to free us and restore joy. Job teaches us that we can open ourselves up to God. We can be vulnerable. God will reveal His character to us in ways we never knew.

As we look at the view of suffering from Satan's vantage point, we might get angry and possibly blame God for not protecting us. Or, we can choose to believe God is absolutely in control and has a purpose for our pain. When we go through a particular trial, we should ask God if His intention is:

- **Corrective?** *"Before I was afflicted I went astray, but now I obey your word"* (Psalm 119:67).
- **Routine?** *"Mankind heads for sin and misery as predictably as flames shoot upwards from a fire"* (Job 5:7, TLB).
- **Designed to glorify Jesus?** *"I am in pain and distress; I will praise God's name in song and glorify him with thanksgiving (Psalm 69:29-30). ". . . this happened so that the work of God might be displayed in his life" (John 9:3).*

God is not finished with us. He's still molding us (Philippians 1:6). No trial comes except by His permission for some wise and loving purpose. God doesn't owe us an explanation. We must trust Him even when we don't understand.

Putting our trust in God is like being awake during surgery. This can be a painful process, and there's no anesthesia. The only anesthesia is trust— trust in the Surgeon. He *is* in complete control. For the short span of our life on earth, we have the extraordinary privilege of being wide-awake as God continues to mold and fashion our characters.

Day Five: Calvary's Love

Jesus didn't come just to rescue us from hell; He came to rescue us from a life of hell on earth. –Sheila Walsh

It's been paid for.

I was sitting in a restaurant, eating my dinner, when a drunkard came in and ordered a sandwich. When the waiter gave him the check and asked him to pay, he said he didn't have the money. The waiter was infuriated because he had to pay for the drunkard's sandwich. He got so mad he started beating him up. One patron yelled, "Leave him alone! I'll pay for his sandwich." The drunkard dragged himself up and said, "Keep your money, you don't have to pay. I just did." At that moment, I witnessed "the blood of the cross."

Jesus paid for us the way the drunkard paid for his sandwich with bruises and blood. Our beloved Savior, Jesus, paid with His life. He submitted to the scourging (whipping, flogging, lashes, beatings, bruises) of His tormentors. As Jesus hung nailed to that cross, He already knew about the messes we'd create in our lives. He says, "You don't have to pay, I already did."

The Secret to Healing

There are no easy answers to suffering. We're often advised, *Buck up! Get a grip.* The only way to get a grip is through the cross. What does the cross really mean?

The answer, in part, is that the cross never promises to free us from pain and suffering. In fact, the cross promises just the opposite; it promises certainty of pain. You say, "I don't want it then!" Listen on. If we're going to learn to deal with our suffering and hurts God's way, then we must come to know that Jesus is our refuge.

When Christ left heaven for earth, He became a faithful High Priest who completely understands our human condition. He came down and got dirty so we could become clean and pure. Like us, Jesus got hungry, tired, and thirsty. He faced temptation and betrayal, "For we do not have a high priest who is unable to sympathize with our weaknesses, but we have one who has been tempted in every way, just as we are—yet was without sin" (Hebrews 4:15). *He knows how we feel.*

Jesus is a touchable God. When He walked among us, He healed the sick and the demon-possessed. When He went to Calvary, He healed all of us—all of our sins—through His death on the cross. And He defeated the devil. Isaiah 53:4 tells us that Jesus *"took up our infirmities [our grief, pain] and carried our sorrows* [sickness], *yet we considered him stricken by God, smitten by him, and afflicted."* Focus on the Healer, not the healing. Think about that.

The Cross Heals

The reason God became man in the person of Jesus was to die for our sins. *God would die for your sin before He'd let you die in your sin.* Sin wounds. The cross heals! The cross is the place God has chosen for us to come to Him in humble faith and obedience. We lay down our pride in order to be forgiven, and are delivered from the punishment we rightly deserve.

Isaiah 53:5–6 reads,

> *"He* [Jesus] *was pierced for our transgressions* [violation of a law or a duty or moral principle], *he was crushed for our iniquities* [immoral act; a sin]; *the punishment that brought us peace was upon him, and by his wounds we are healed. We all, like sheep, have gone astray, each of us has turned to his own way; and the Lord has laid on him[self] the iniquity* [sin] *of us all."*

"By his wounds we are healed." Healed of what? Scripture can help us interpret Scripture. 1 Peter 2:24–25 reads:

> *"He himself bore our sins in his body on the tree, so that we might die to sins and live for righteousness; by his wounds you have been healed. For you were like sheep going astray, but now you have returned to the Shepherd and Overseer of your souls."*

According to these passages, the cross was God's means of saving us from sin so we could live righteous lives (the opposite of sin is righteous). Our slates have been wiped clean. *Those shameful and destructive secrets have been nailed to Christ's cross.* The real body makeover we need is forgiveness of our sins.

Through God's provision we can put away all our painful masks. Colossians 3:1–5 gives us the key to freedom:

> *"Since, then, you have been raised with Christ, set your hearts on things above, where Christ is seated at the right hand of God. Set your minds on things above, not on earthly things. For you died, and your life is now hidden with Christ in God. When Christ, who is your life, appears, then you also will appear with him in glory. Put to death, therefore, whatever belongs to your earthly nature: sexual immorality, impurity, lust, evil desires and greed, which is idolatry."*

No matter what's happened in our past, we can live without possessiveness, anger, hate, bitterness, jealousy, and envy. We can live a life free from perfection, free from that which causes distortment of our body image, and ultimately destruction. The starting point is setting our hearts and minds on the things above.

The Reward

The message of the cross is about the power of God, and that Christ is the power and the wisdom of God (see 1 Corinthians 1:18, 24). We must intentionally focus on Jesus Christ and continually remind ourselves *we are forgiven of every sinful act and desire. We are no longer enslaved by sin.* Once Jesus Christ becomes our Savior, we confess our sins. "Confess" means to tell God and bring out into the open. Then God *does not see* our past anymore. It's been completely erased. He gets very excited for our future.

Each one of us has been searching for the secret to healing and restoration. This is it! *You've just unlocked the mystery behind returning to a normal life—a new normal!* This is a free gift. You're already in—it's not through some secretive initiation or application process but rather through what Christ has already done for you. God has raised you from the dead as He did Christ. When you were stuck in your old sin-dead life, you were incapable of responding to God. *God has now brought you back to life.* When He hung on the cross, He said, *"It's finished"* (John 19:30).

Closing Moments

Jesus understands *every* struggle.

Jesus was tempted in every way we are (but He did not sin). So, whenever we're struggling, we can come bravely before the throne of God to receive mercy and grace to help us in our time of need (Hebrews 4:16). In times of darkness, we are safe in Him.

We might think seriously about these words of Socrates, especially if we compare ourselves to others and desire to trade places, "If all our misfortunes were laid in one common heap whence everyone must take an equal portion, most people would be content to take their own and depart." We should remember that the problems before us are *never* bigger than the Power behind us. Regardless of how dark it seems right now, there is an end in sight! *"When the earth and all its people quake, it's I [God] who hold its pillars firm"* (Psalm 75:3).

Promise to Claim: "Heal me, O Lord, and I will be healed; save me and I will be saved, for you are the one I praise." (Jeremiah 17:14)

Week 3

The Beauty of Truth

Who is the fairest of them all?

Fat, ugly, unloved, wrinkled, and worthless. This is often what we think as we look in the mirror. There are days when we feel ugly no matter how much time we put into looking good. Some days we feel like mistakes dressing up as people. Criticizing ourselves on the outside is usually caused by the way we feel inside. When we measure ourselves by our physical appearance, we'll always feel let down.

No one can always be the fairest of them all. No-body is perfect.

Everyone wants to feel attractive and loved. The problem is the more we focus on what we look like on the outside, the less fulfillment and joy comes from the inside. I know. I've tried it. Blinded to the beauty God planned for my life, my search railroaded me off His super-highway onto an empty, unfulfilling gravel road filled with potholes.

I hope you're beginning to understand that your real glow comes from the inside. An old Danish proverb goes, "What you are is God's gift to you. What you do with yourself is your gift to God." God gave every one of us gifts, talents, and passions, but we've buried them under our issues and habits. Corrie ten Boom wisely stated, "Every experience God gives us, every person He puts in our lives is the perfect preparation for the future that only He can see." God created you on purpose for a distinct reason. Accept yourself as a beautiful person inside and out. You make mistakes, but you are not a mistake!

God is waiting for you to say the words, "Papa, I need your love and gracious fatherly care. I want to claim my royal inheritance and status as your daughter. Enable me to live as your beloved child—one who knows without a shadow of a doubt that I belong to you."

Day One: Conquer Fear

I misjudged you. At first I thought you were a mover and a shaker. Now I see you were just trembling. –Unknown

Fear is immobilizing.

Jessica wrote, "Fear has permeated every part of my life. Fear of being punished by God for what I've done and for not letting Him into my life. Fear for my health. Fear of losing my job. Fear that what I believe about myself is true. Fear that my children will grow up and resent me. Fear that my marriage will fail. Fear that people will learn the ugly truth about me. Fear that I'll never get better because I'm beyond repair. Fear that this pain will never end. Fear that my life will come to a tragic end."

Fear must be endemic because almost every book in the Bible has a "fear not" verse in it. Each angelic appearance begins with the same three words: "Do not fear." Jesus said, *"Live in me. Make your home in me just as I do in you" (John 15:4, MSG).* Jesus is inviting us to inhabit a new space in which we can live without fear and anxiety.

What Do I Fear?

The collapse of the German Berlin Wall in 1989 was monumental because it represented the end of an era—the end of division, captivity, and fear. Many believed the wall would never come down. I think of fear as a great wall which divides because it encourages fear, isolation, and imprisonment.

A big component of the pain we feel is fear—fear this obsession may never go away, like an unmoving cloud cover. What do you fear today? Change, God, gaining weight, losing weight, rejection, relapsing, imperfection, disapproval, therapy, medication, a strict new regime, being judged, restoring broken relationships, or a whole new lifestyle?

The first thing you must remember is that God created us with the capacity to fear. Properly controlled, fear can protect us and motivate us to positive action. Uncontrolled toxic fear can imprison us and stunt our personal and spiritual growth.

What happens if we let toxic fear control us? Fear will:

- Immobilize us and enslave us.

- Open the door for the work of Satan (leading to sin).
- Cause physical problems.
- Bring shame, confusion, and isolation.
- Cause us to abandon relationships and focus on ourselves.
- Keep us from knowing and serving God.
- Usurp our God-given passion and be a roadblock to our destiny.

The enemy uses fear, but God asks us to have faith in Him, and to give Him all our anxieties. *"Perfect love casts out fear"* (1 John 4:18). God's love for us and our faith in Him removes fear. The Bible lists many failures and fears of spiritual leaders to us show the love and strength of God, not people.

Fear doesn't have to be a life sentence! You can push those walls down in the name of Jesus. To get a proper perspective on your fear: One, recognize Jesus challenges us to have faith to conquer fear (Matthew 21:21–22). He's in the middle of it and knows all about it. Focus on Him, not the issue. Two, focus on God's promises such as:

- *"The Lord is my light and my salvation. Who is there to fear? The Lord is my life's fortress. Who is there to be afraid of?"* (Psalm 27:1)

- *"You will not leave in haste or go in flight; for the Lord will go before you, the God of Israel will be your rear guard"* (Isaiah 52:12). We can be free from fear by remembering God has us completely covered!

- *"Be strong and courageous. Do not be afraid or terrified because of them, for the LORD your God goes with you; he will never leave you nor forsake you. The LORD himself goes before you and will be with you; he will never leave you nor forsake you. Do not be afraid; do not be discouraged"* (Deuteronomy 31:6, 8).

When God says, "Do not fear," He's giving us a word of comfort—a specific promise of His presence with us. He will *not* fail us. There will always be a "them" in our lives, whether it is a group of people or our own self-condemning voices. Why do you think God mentioned twice that He'd never abandon us?

Fear of Man

Many of our behaviors come out of the need for approval from another person, which is really fear—fear of man. Most of us name our number one fear as "what others will think about me." To "fear man" can go one of two ways. One, we can become so obsessed with another person we're in awe of them, possibly codependent. This is idolatry. Or two, the person's opinion of us is so important we become afraid of the consequences of this person not approving of us. This type of fear is debilitating.

Proverbs 29:25 says, *"Fear of man will prove to be a snare, but whoever trusts in the LORD is kept safe."* If you look at Jesus's life and teaching, He didn't need to create an impression. His thought process and messages were completely God-directed. He never compromised. He feared no human being. Many people asked Jesus to do things for them, but He always considered what God desired, even if it meant disappointing people (Mark 1:29-38, John 11:1-6).

Remember, God commands us to get together with His people. If you fear this kind of commitment, *focus on Him.* Say, "I will be obedient and go to this gathering regardless of my feelings. God's Word says, *"In God I trust; I will not be afraid. What can man do to me?"* (Psalm 56:11)

Our best option is to immobilize fear with faith. Fear is a very uncomfortable emotion. It is the enemy of faith. 2 Timothy 1:7 says that God did not give us a spirit of fearfulness, but a spirit of power, of love, and of self-discipline and a sound mind. This means that any fear, any shaken confidence like rejection, comes from Satan. And Satan has *no* power over Christians. We have the authority to tell him to leave us alone. Say, "Satan, it's written [*for example*] the LORD will protect me from all evil; He has preserved my soul" (paraphrase; Psalm 121:7).

Healthy Fear

Let's not overlook the good kind of fear which is God-given. All people have an instinctual response to potential danger, which is important to survival. It motivates us to buy home insurance (fear of fire), to follow the law (fear of prison), and to obey (fear of discipline).

One other kind of fear is healthy: fear of the Lord, which means "to have a reverential awe of." Biblically, "to fear the Lord" means we hold Him up in reverence and with respect because He is so awesome and holy; therefore, we obey and trust Him. Scripture says, *"The fear of the LORD is the beginning of knowledge" (Proverbs 1:7).*

Day Two: Our Toxic Emotions

God knows exactly where to meet you. –My friend Edie

Depression is a household word today.

Every woman has for a time felt down in the dumps and experienced loss of some kind. Adversity is a normal part of life. Yet, sometimes we sink in quicksand and we can't get out. We can't pull ourselves out because life feels too hard. Depression and anxiety are rampant in America today. One in four women will experience at least one episode of depression in her lifetime. Some women experience many episodes. [9]

Laura writes, "I feel myself slipping into a self-absorbed, secluded world. I'm shutting people out. I could break down in floods of tears at any moment. I feel so fragile and insignificant and a nuisance. I'm angry with everybody. I just want to be by myself. My head is such a mess. I'm confused and incredibly depressed."

Depression can be brought on by biochemistry, or a significant loss, or illness. When we lose the ability to enjoy things, or feel bad about and blame ourselves, or feel guilty for no reason, believing we don't deserve to be happy, this is when we're likely to experience depression.

Depression goes beyond the blues. To be depressed is to be "pressed or cast down." There are various reasons we direct our emotions down or inward—abuse, loss of a loved one, stress, pursuit of thinness, guilt, intense teasing, and/or rejection. Depression can also be a symptom of unbelief.

The Bible is full of people with broken hearts and spirits. In the first chapter of 1 Samuel, Hannah, a godly woman, became depressed when she had to deal with a combination of unfulfilled longings and a strained relationship. She had a godly husband, Elkanah, who loved her dearly. However, for reasons known only to the Lord, she was unable to bear children.

Hannah's struggles with barrenness were exacerbated by her husband's second wife, Peninnah. She had no difficulty conceiving children. She "kept provoking Hannah in order to irritate her." For years, she aggravated Hannah until she wept and couldn't eat. Hannah experienced severe depression.

Provoked by Penny's malice, Hannah refused to retaliate. Instead she poured out her heart and soul to God. Her ally Eli said, "Go in peace, and may the God of Israel grant you what you have asked of him." Hannah went her way and was no longer downcast. She joined in the worship of the Lord in the morning. Her prayers were answered in time—in God's time. She conceived and gave birth to a son, Samuel.

You may feel pressed or cast down but you have the power to pick up your sword and wield it at the evil one. Remind him of Revelation 12:10: "Now is come salvation, and strength, and the kingdom of our God, and the power of his Christ: for the accuser of our brethren is cast down."

Isolation and Connection

Imagine what it would be like to be a prisoner sentenced to solitary confinement. It's dark, cold, as close to living in a coffin as you can come. There's no way out. Only loneliness. Only darkness. Addiction and depression usually leads to isolation.

Today, you may feel like you're in solitary confinement. That's not a good feeling, is it? This is because God did not design us to be isolated. We were created in His image, made to have a relationship with Him and other people. However, many of us have become that prisoner in solitary confinement. When we isolate ourselves from God and others, it's impossible to feel joy.

I'd decline social invitations in lieu of a binge, and after a while, people just stopped inviting me out. I stole hundreds of hours from my employer when I left my sales territory early to go home and binge—alone. The guilt and loneliness re-fueled the depression. One day, my boyfriend told me I needed to make more friends because I was "smothering" him. He was right. I began reconnecting with the world, slowly but surely . . . and it felt good!

God knows about our emotional isolation and He answers our prayers by offering opportunities for connection with others. Encouraging one another helps to break down the walls. Hebrews 3:13 says, "Encourage one another daily, as long as it's called Today, so that none of you may be hardened by sin's deceitfulness." Don't miss God's divine appointment set up just for you!

I'm Guilty!

Let me count the ways I feel guilty! I felt a tremendous amount of guilt when I skipped classes in college (an education my parents worked hard to pay for) to binge. Due to a hangover, I no-showed for two weddings. Is it any wonder I had few friends? I felt tremendous guilt over giving two decades of my life to addiction.

When a person rides the roller coaster of dieting, exercising, bingeing, starving, then feelings of failure surface which lead to feelings of guilt and self-condemnation. In Psalm 38:4–11, David describes his guilt. His words paint a picture of the consequences of not dealing with these emotions. Check the ones you have personally experienced.

- Verse 4: "My guilt has overwhelmed me like a burden too
- heavy to bear."
- Verse 5: "My wounds fester and are loathsome because of my sinful folly."
- Verse 6: "I am bowed down and brought very low; all day long I go about mourning."
- Verse 7: "My back is filled with searing pain; there is no health in my body."
- Verse 8: "I am feeble and utterly crushed; I groan in anguish of heart."
- Verse 9: "All my longings lie open before you, O Lord; my sighing is not hidden from you."
- Verse 10: "My heart pounds, my strength fails me; even the light has gone from my eyes."
- Verse 11: "My friends and companions avoid me because of my wounds; my neighbors stay far away."

Many of us feel guilty for wasting valuable years focusing on ourselves and our obsessions when we could have been participating in life nurturing experiences. The good news is we can relieve and wash away our guilt. Psalm 32:5 tells us how,

"I acknowledged my sin to you and did not cover up my iniquity. I said, "I will confess my transgressions [sin or wrongdoings] *to the Lord"—and you forgave the guilt of my sin."*

God wants us to give Him all our guilt.

My Name is Shame

After the fourth flush I grabbed the near empty bottle of *Windex*, then ripped off three squares of paper toweling and proceeded to clean up around the toilet bowl. After tossing the residue of a gaping emotional wound into the garbage I reclined on the couch, numb and oblivious. *I feel like garbage . . . but tomorrow will be different*, I promised myself. *Today is the last day.*

Driven by shame, it never was the last day. Dr. Larry Crabb wrote,

"The real killer of the self and the real cause of all addictions is shame. Shame is the experience of feeling deficient. Shame causes us to see our identity as flawed rather than seeing ourselves as having flaws. Our harsh judgments lead us to see ourselves as ugly, stupid, and fat. The result is a deep hole in the soul."[10]

Most of us are ashamed of our behavior. I'd regularly berate myself because no normal person would put herself through this sort of monstrous ritual. How could even God love someone who does such things? I didn't tell anyone for fear of rejection and embarrassment. We work to hide our behavior because we're afraid of the answer to "the question," *Will you still love me now that you know?*

There are two kinds of shame: shame that comes from another's actions, and shame that comes from our personal actions. Jesus said, *"The things that come out of the mouth come from the heart, and these make a man 'unclean'"* *(Matthew 15:18)*. In other words, nothing *outside a person* can render him or her unclean. Food can't; people can't; the sins of your family can't; perpetrators can't. Get out of your mind that you're dirty, or can be contaminated by coming into contact with someone you define as unclean, or by not measuring up to society's standards.

Nobody can make you an untouchable outcast.

According to Scripture, evil thoughts, murder, adultery, sexual sins, stealing, lying, and cursing come from within ourselves (Matthew 15:17-19). When we do sin, God is quick to forgive when we turn to him. No one else has the power to make us sin. This is why we're counseled to transform our minds, which ultimately translates into purer actions. When our insides are clean, then our outsides are clean.

Serita Ann Jakes said, "Deliverance finally comes when you confront your past and put it in its proper perspective. It happened to you but it's not you. You survived the trauma; you too can walk again."

Day Three: Lies versus Truths

Truth is like surgery—it may hurt, but it heals. –Unknown

"God's Word is truth" (John 17:17).

Most of us, to some degree, have old tapes that replay in our minds— voices that are critical and condemning. *Who do you think you are to … Don't do this or you'll . . . You cannot . . .* These toxic tapes enslave us. You're not alone. Our insecurities are universal.

Did you know that when you believe a lie you break your circles of love and trust; that when lies take up residence they wound your soul? Every lie is a set up for a new wound. How does a lie do that? It masquerades as truth.

How then do we heal and restore our circles of love and trust? Truth. And it begins with the truth about God. These voices are not from God. He speaks with gentleness and compassion. He speaks only truth, not lies.

Truth destroys lies and restores trust. Jesus said, *"I am the way and the truth and the life"* (John 14:6). Truth is powerful and is available to anyone who seeks it in Jesus Christ. We must believe what the late theologian Francis Schaeffer called the *true* truth: the truth that comes from God and is found only in His Word. This is how we live free.

The opposite of truth is a *lie:* "a false statement deliberately presented as being true; a falsehood; something meant to deceive or give a wrong impression."[11] Denial is a lie.

Here is another illustration describing how Satan traps and lies to us (a paraphrase of *The Screwtapes Letters* by C. S. Lewis):

My Dear Followers,

The following instructions shall help you handicap female believers and convince them to come on our side. One of our greatest allies at present is her perception of herself. It's your task, therefore, to feed her poor self-esteem. Already she wastes time primping in front of the mirror and worrying about her looks.

Continue to encourage her to compare herself to those whom she admires. This will eventually immobilize her. When she feels inadequate, she'll no longer attempt anything for Christ's kingdom because of her fear of failure. Her warped self-image will lead to unhealthy relationships and hinder her ability to love others. The more she tells herself that she's a bad person and not competent, the more easily she'll feel threatened by others. This will turn others off to Christ and his loathsome Christianity.

Finally, emphasize her weaknesses so that she begins to believe that she's unimportant to Christ. This will push her to compulsive striving to please him through her own accomplishments. Her works will no longer be motivated by faith, but by a dislike for herself. Confuse her so she'll never feel forgiven. If you successfully convince her that Christ is never pleased with her, she'll grow weary and give up altogether.[12]

This is what Satan does to us. He deceives us. We hate ourselves, become embittered to others, and blame others. He uses other people's remarks to hurt us or create fear in our hearts. This happens because we never were told the truth. The truth is:

- *"Your enemy the devil prowls around like a roaring lion looking for someone to devour"* *(1 Peter 5:8)*.
- *"He is a thief that comes only to steal and kill and destroy"* *(John 10:10)*.

Few of us consider the consequences of our choices. Look at me. I saw beautiful, thin women being paraded around telling me this is what I had to look like. Because my body and beauty weren't naturally like a super-model's, I made some bad choices trying to attain that look. At the time, these choices seemed acceptable. An innocent babe, I ended up trapped for over twenty years. I cared more about looking like a model than pleasing my Father, my Creator. Get ready to let go of the lies that hold you captive!

How Did This All Start?

Early church father, John Chrysostom, said, "God, having placed good and evil in our power, has given us full freedom of choice."

Satan's lie was the starting place for all the trouble in this world (see Genesis 3). Satan's objective was to drive a wedge between God and His first children, Adam and Eve. He knew they wouldn't deliberately go against God, so he subtly tricked them with a reasonable and desirable offer.

Satan deceived Eve through a clever combination of outright lies disguised as truth. He began by planting seeds of doubt in her mind. He suggested God had said something He hadn't said. The truth is that God said they were free to eat from any tree in the garden except one, *"Do not eat from the tree of the knowledge of good and evil for when you eat of it you will surely die" (Genesis 2:17).*

Satan countered with, *"You will not surely die . . . For God knows that when you eat of it your eyes will be opened, and you will be like God, knowing good and evil."*

Satan deceived Eve by causing her to question God's love and motives. *"Did God really say, 'You must not eat from any tree in the garden?'"*

In other words, *That's a lie! You won't die! God knows very well that the instant you eat it, you'll become like him! You deserve this!* What an offer! For the first time in history, a lie was spoken (and the couple eventually died).

Scripture says, *"Then the Lord God said to the woman, 'What is this you have done?' The woman said, 'The serpent deceived me, and I ate.'"* From that moment to today, Satan has used deception to influence our choices, win our love, and destroy our lives. Satan uses similar reasoning with us as he tempts us to water down God's Word. He tells us to make our own choices, choices that appear sensible. Instead of asking, "God, did you really say?" We think we know what we need, and so we move forward on our own and state, "God did not really say."

Satan's Disguises

Satan doesn't appear in the form of a serpent today. Often, he comes as an erotic romance novel, through celebrity or a movie, soap opera, advertisement, or a song. He may also pose as someone giving sincere counsel. Anytime we receive input *inconsistent with the Word of God*, we can be sure Satan is trying to deceive us. What we read or hear may sound, feel, and seem right, but if it's contrary to God's Word, it isn't right.

How did we fall into his trap? Romans 1:25 explains, "They exchanged the truth of God for a lie, and worshiped and served created things (idols) rather than the Creator."

First, Satan plants the lie. Then we listen to the lie and dwell on it. We begin to follow what Satan has placed in our minds. We contemplate that this feels or sounds right, so we believe the lie. We rationalize it, then consent and act on the lie. Our beliefs get stronger that produce behavior, which in our case is destructive, sinful behavior.

Sin always affects others, just as it did with Adam and Eve. The Bible tells of God's plan to restore the fallen image. It's the story of God working to break through to human beings in order to restore what had been lost. He's doing it with us right now.

Day Four: Who Am I?

The soul will not be healed without truth. –Dr. Larry Crabb

Bondage begins with a lie.

Satan throws out the bait—images of the perfect body and woman. We eat it and he reels us in. He cunningly convinced us his ideas were the right ones. We never saw the hook—the lie. The Bible says, *"Truth is nowhere to be found . . ." (Isaiah 59:15).* The word "truth" appears more than 224 times in the Bible. We must address the lies that put us in bondage and replace them with the truth.

Think of it this way. Your mind is like a computer. In your computer, you've probably got years of data collected. In your mind, you have years of rejection, hurt, deception, and anger programmed—*years of accusations and lies.* You made a choice: to believe the data or not; to delete the data or not.

We must directly battle Satan's lies and confusion with truth. The truth will set us free. It's been said that Satan trembles when he sees the weakest saint upon his knees submitting to Jesus. This isn't because he's afraid of us. It is because he knows the power of God gives us victory over the works of darkness—of accusations and lies.

A. W. Tozer said that if the devil comes to you and whispers that you are no good, don't argue with him, instead, remind him:

"Regardless of what you say about me, I must tell you how the Lord feels about me. He tells me that I am so valuable to him that he gave himself for me on the cross!"[13]

The Truth Will Set Me Free!

The human mind is like a computer. It mirrors the information we feed it. Proverbs 23:7 captures this idea when it says, *"As he thinks in his heart, so is he."* We become what we think about. The antidote for deception is truth. This is why the Bible says to keep our thoughts on whatever is true.

We know that those who meditate over and speak God's Word's out loud tend to change their thinking and habits faster. *Truth changes our thinking, and thinking changes our behavior.* As you recognize a lie, defend yourself out loud—and often. Repetition aids in reprogramming negative self-talk. Say: *I'm perfect just the way I am!* Achieving a new way of life consists of repeating positive actions.

Second Corinthians 10:5 tells us to take captive every thought and make it obedient to Christ. To "take every thought captive" means refusing to allow other people's approval or disapproval of me dominate my thinking. When we have that toxic thought, we shout "Stop!" and we give it to Jesus to dispose of. Go through the following list and find the statements that best describe you. Then speak it out loud in your own words from your heart. This is called *positive self-talk* or *affirmations.*

Corrupt Data: I'm fat.
Speak it out: I'm just the perfect size! I'm fearfully and wonderfully made!
God's Word: Psalm 139:14; 1 Peter 3:3–4

Corrupt Data: I'm dumb and stupid.
Speak it out: I have the mind of Christ!
God's Word: 1 Corinthians 2:16

Corrupt Data: I'm ugly.
Speak it out: I'm beautiful and made in God's image!
God's Word: Genesis 1:27

Corrupt Data: Nothing I've tried works. I'm weak and a lost cause.
Speak it out: I'm strong!
God's Word: 2 Corinthians 12:9; Joel 3:10

Corrupt Data: I'm lost. I don't know how to get back to normal.
Speak it out: God has a plan for my life! I'm found!
God's Word: Psalm 23:1–4; Luke 15:6; Jeremiah 29:11

Corrupt Data: I'm a victim of my past and always will be.
Speak it out: I'm a victor!
God's Word: Psalm 60:12; 1 Corinthians 15:57

Corrupt Data: I'm worthless.
Speak it out: I'm treasured!
God's Word: Deuteronomy 7:6

Corrupt Data: I'm so scared.
Speak it out: I'm safe!
God's Word: Proverbs 18:10; Psalm 3:3

Corrupt Data: I can never be healed and don't deserve to be healed.
Speak it out: God is my Healer! I'm healed!
God's Word: Isaiah 53:5; Exodus 15:26

Corrupt Data: I cannot!
Speak it out: I can do all things through Christ who strengthens me!
God's Word: Philippians 4:13

Corrupt Data: I'm not worthy of being loved.
Speak it out: God loves me unconditionally!
 God's Word: John 15:9

Corrupt Data: I've been addicted to food for too long. I'll never be free.
Speak it out: The Spirit lives in me. I'm free!
God's Word: 2 Corinthians 3:17

Corrupt Data: No one likes me. You wouldn't like me.
Speak it out: My worth is in who God says I am!
God's Word: Psalm 8:5–8

These are God's Words. Plug into His Word every day. Not only will you begin to see the truth, but your faith will grow stronger. You'll find that over time, your spiritual muscles of resisting Satan will grow, and the battle will get easier.

Speak it out: I'm beautiful! I'm lovable! I'm worthy. I'm capable! I'm not just saying that—God says that. Praise God! You have just taken off and destroyed your masks!

The Conflict Zones

In every Christian's life there's a certain amount of tension. When we become Christians, I wish I could say life on earth is like living in the Garden of Eden. There are periodic walks through the valley of darkness. There's tension. Paul describes it as a war, a battle for control. We can expect conflict to arise in three areas of our lives:

- *The world*: A societal system of ungodly and unhealthy sets of values and morals.
- *The spiritual realm*: Unseen warfare with Satan and his demons.
- *Within ourselves:* Our carnal nature or sinful flesh.

Our minds and hearts are the battleground where conflict with these enemies are either won or lost. It can be very hard to discern when our struggles are a result of the devil's intervention, us acting in our flesh, environmental and cultural pressures, or even abnormal brain physiology, or hormonal changes. These three negative influences commonly work together to lead us away from God. Most often we aren't even aware this is happening.

Do you want a God-extreme makeover—to overcome and live a victorious life free from the power and pollution of sin? You can! It's called *sanctification*—the process of growing more into the image of Christ and being increasingly enabled to live rightly, while releasing the reigns of sin. When we were saved (salvation) we gave *our sin* to God. When we begin sanctification, we give *ourselves* to God.

What we're learning to do is surrender ourselves to God's process of sanctification. We begin by drawing power from Christ himself. *"You will understand the incredible greatness of God's power for us who believe him. This is the same mighty power which raised Christ from the dead"* (Ephesians 1:19-20, NLT).

Day Five: Arm Yourself for Spiritual Warfare

Don't let us yield to temptation, but rescue us from the evil one.
—Jesus, speaking in Matthew 6:13 (NLT)

Be aware! Stand guard! Get armed!

Satan will want to cloud your mind as you study the truth. His goal is to take our minds and hearts off Jesus Christ, then steer us into the world's practices. Jesus can help us because He was tempted by Satan.

Luke 4:1–12 tells us:

"Jesus, full of the Holy Spirit, returned from the Jordan and was led by the Spirit in the desert, where for forty days he was tempted by the devil. He ate nothing during those days, and at the end of them he was hungry. The devil said to him, "If you are the Son of God, tell this stone to become bread." Jesus answered, "It's written: 'Man does not live on bread alone.'"

"The devil led him up to a high place and showed him in an instant all the kingdoms of the world. And he said to him, "I will give you all their authority and splendor, for it has been given to me, and I can give it to anyone I want to. So if you worship me, it will all be yours." Jesus answered, "It's written: Worship the Lord your God and serve him only."

"The devil led him to Jerusalem and had him stand on the highest point of the temple. "If you are the Son of God," he said, "throw yourself down from here. For its written: "He will command his angels concerning you to guard you carefully; they will lift you up in their hands, so that you will not strike your foot against a stone." Jesus answered, "It says: 'Do not put the Lord your God to the test'."

Satan first tried to get Jesus to slip by appealing to His need to relieve His hunger. Similarly, we're most tempted to slip back into our old behaviors and addictions when we're hungry, angry, lonely, tired, or depressed. With each temptation Satan offered, Jesus resisted him with the power of the Word of God: "It is written . . ." It was imprinted on His heart. When we wield God's truth back at Satan, we win.

As Satan tempts us, we must fight with God's Word: "It's written . . ." Notice that Jesus's response was low key. There was no wielding of swords or summoning angelic beings to fight. He used the simple, direct proclamation of the powerful living Word of God.

There is another truth I want to point out. Satan said, *"If you are the Son of God . . ."* This is another phrase Satan casually slips into our minds: *If you really are . . . Who are you to . . .* Jesus was secure in His identity. We must be too. We tell him, "I am redeemed by the blood of Christ . . . I am adopted into God's family . . . I am loved ecstatically by God Almighty!"

Luke 4:13 says, *"When the devil had finished all this tempting, he left him until an opportune time."* Satan will leave you when you resist him, but *he always comes back.* He waits for just the right moment. Satan persisted in his attempts to get Jesus off track. We'll not find immunity either.

Remember, God alone holds your destiny. Satan's time is limited, and his destiny has already been decided. John said, *"The prince of this world, shall be cast out" (John 12:31).* Our attitude must be, "I cannot defeat the devil, but I can resist him and trust Jesus to defeat him for me."

God wants us to be wise, aware, informed, and ready. James 4:7 tells us how to arm ourselves: "Submit yourselves, then, to God. Resist the devil, and he will flee from you." Notice the order in which you are to act—submit first, resist second. The word "submit" means to line up under another's authority. When we line up under God's authority we're not alone. God is standing beside us. He is far mightier than the enemy.

Closing Moments

Keeping secrets always leads to unhappiness.

We've tried to hide our secrets from God and others. The isolation, guilt, shame, and grief is too much to bear. The only way for us to find freedom is to confess our wrongs to God and seek a new life through Him. We have all heard the saying, "Confession is good for the soul." There is healing power in confession. It's a process of becoming open, real, and honest with God, with others, and ourselves.

As we turn our life over to God, Satan will most likely bring lying thoughts into our minds to make us fearful of surrendering. He'll say if we give control to God, then we'll relinquish joy in our life. Not true! God is not in the business of condemning His children—that's Satan's business. God's business is to free us and draw us closer to Him. My life is complete, fun, and full of joy now that I've given myself to the Lord. Satan won for a long time because I was blind to his tactics. Part of our new life requires becoming wise to Satan's games and strategies.

Nothing less than the "God of all comfort" can meet our deepest needs. We're not merely fighting against food, behavior patterns, substances, or dysfunctional people. We're fighting an enemy. When Satan is knocking at your door, simply say, "Jesus, could You get that for me?" Those that succeed gain victory in prayer long before the battle begins.

My advice is to pray a "Warrior's Prayer" every morning:

"God, Help me to remember as I face life's challenges that an unseen war is going on for my spiritual life. Send your Holy Spirit to give me the wisdom to recognize what is the truth and what is a lie. Remind me that the best way to win the battles of my mind is in prayer and by reading your Word. Thank you for assuring me of victory today. I surrender all to you and let you fight for me. By faith, I claim victory over my life! Nothing can hurt me. In Jesus's name, Amen."

Promise to Claim: "If you hold to my [Jesus] teaching, you are really my disciples. Then you will know the truth, and the truth will set you free." (John 8:31–32)

Week 4

Anger is a Choice

Resentment. Grudges. Bitterness.

Many of our emotions have an anger component to them. Nearly every woman I know who struggles with her image and worth feels these emotions—and is held captive to them when left unresolved. As women, we learn to silence our anger, to deny it entirely, or to vent it in a way that leaves us feeling helpless and powerless. We can suppress it, deny it, allow it to control us . . . or learn to overcome it.

Anger is powerful and it is God-given. The dictionary defines it: "a strong feeling of displeasure or hostility." Anger is an inward emotion caused by an outward action, circumstance, or situation. This action, circumstance, or situation may be something we do, or it may be something done apart from us, or done to us. When it arises, we respond.

These emotions just don't go away. Anger is either directed outward, inward, or projected onto others. Denied, anger expresses itself in symptoms like depression, obsession, and overeating. Your issues with food and self-image may be a symptom of anger. You may not even recognize you have stored up that much emotion. Sometime and somewhere in the past, you were deeply hurt by someone or something. We tend to turn that hurt inward and stuff it with food or other objects. Psychologist Gregory Jantz said,

> "For some reason you couldn't direct that anger at the person responsible for your pain, so it stayed within you. Anger, improperly directed and unexpressed leads to resentment. Resentment has festered into self-destructive eating. Confronting your anger and those who caused it will free you for the next step, forgiveness."[14]

The good news is that anger channeled positively can be a gift. Think of it like a gas flame on a stovetop. The flame isn't destructive when it's used properly. Used correctly, the flame is a good thing for cooking our food. Used improperly, the flame can be harmful and destructive. We can learn to express anger in healthy ways.

Note: There is 6 days this week and slightly more work because uncovering anger is so critical to healing. I encourage you to put more time aside for this very important lesson.

Day One: God's Anger

When a train goes through a tunnel and it gets dark, you don't throw away the ticket and jump off. You sit still and trust the engineer. —Corrie Ten Boom

God gets angry too.

Ellie is mad at her dad for bringing her up in bars and then turning his back when her uncle raped her, resulting in pregnancy. Today, seventeen years later, Ellie loses control in fits of rage and manages to destroy everything good in her life. Jana is angry because her father left unannounced one day, abandoning his family. These women's anger is justified. More importantly, it makes God angry too.

Over time, these women came to forgive their fathers. Consequently, God has done some miraculous things in their lives. Each woman came to terms with her weight and body image. Ellie no longer binges and purges. Jana doesn't diet excessively or overeat anymore. Restoration began when they became willing to give their anger to God.

The Bible is full of examples of anger—constructive and destructive. God was the first person to feel anger when He expelled Adam and Eve from the Garden of Eden. There are many other examples of God expressing His anger (for example, Deuteronomy 29:28, Psalms 78:49 and 90:7).

Yes, our God is the God of unconditional love, but there are things He hates. He hates pride and arrogance, evil behavior, and perverse speech (Proverbs 8:13). Proverbs 6:16–19 list six things the Lord hates; seven that are detestable to Him:

- Haughty (proud, arrogant, overly conceited) eyes.
- A lying tongue.
- Hands that shed innocent blood.
- A heart that devises wicked schemes.
- Feet quick to rush into evil.
- A false witness who pours out lies.
- A man who stirs up dissension among brothers.

Yet, God is slow to anger:

- Psalm 78:38: *"Yet he was merciful; he forgave their iniquities and did not destroy them. Time after time, he restrained his anger and did not stir up his full wrath."*
- Exodus 34:6–7: *"The Lord, the compassionate and gracious God, slow to anger, abounding in love and faithfulness, maintaining love to thousands, and forgiving wickedness, rebellion and sin."*

The difference between God's anger and man's is that God's anger is controlled, with purpose; not uncontrolled. The purpose of His anger is to correct or stop destructive behavior. It is not selfish but an expression of concern. He gets angry at injustice and willful disobedience, not at those who cross Him or seek to take revenge, as man does. One cannot read the Old Testament without seeing God's anger. The good news is as His children we are saved from God's wrath, and we experience His forgiveness through Jesus's work on the cross.

Day Two: Jesus's Anger

He told the dove merchants, "Get your things out of here! Stop turning my Father's house into a shopping mall!"—Jesus, speaking in John 2:16 (MSG)

Jesus Christ, in the flesh, felt anger.

Jesus had the same emotions we do. He became angry when He saw others commit wrongdoings, but He used it to see that justice was served. There were two times that Jesus was righteously angry. Yet, He was righteously controlled. Jesus always handled His anger in a way pleasing to God, because He only said and did things that pleased God. What was the cause of Jesus's anger in John 2:13–16?

"When it was almost time for the Jewish Passover, Jesus went up to Jerusalem. In the temple courts he found men selling cattle, sheep and doves, and others sitting at tables exchanging money. So he made a whip out of cords, and drove all from the temple area, both sheep and cattle; he scattered the coins of the money changers and overturned their tables. To those who sold doves he said, "Get these out of here! How dare you turn my Father's house into a market!""

Jesus revealed His zeal for God by cleansing the temple (cleaning house). Yet He didn't destroy anyone's property. Notice Jesus carefully planned and executed His response. He made it clear He was in command, in complete control. He made a whip out of cords. This is a time-consuming project— time Jesus most likely used to think and control His anger. He never showed selfish induced anger. In Mark 3:1–5, again, Jesus was righteously controlled.

"Another time he went into the synagogue, and a man with a shriveled hand was there. Some of them were looking for a reason to accuse Jesus, so they watched him closely to see if he would heal him on the Sabbath. Jesus said to the man with the shriveled hand, "Stand up in front of everyone." Then Jesus asked them, "Which is lawful on the Sabbath: to do good or to do evil, to save life or to kill?" But they remained silent. He looked around at them in anger and, deeply distressed at their stubborn hearts, said to the man, "Stretch out your hand." He stretched it out, and his hand was completely restored."

Notice Jesus continued with the healing instead of verbally showing distress. He expressed His emotions. Yet, His expression of anger was righteous because He is righteous. Our emotions can be destructive, destroying people, and relationships. However, we can learn to model Jesus. Jesus made use of His anger. He used it against wrong.

When Jesus saw people being victimized by evil of any kind, or saw God's will being thwarted, He got angry. So, it follows that anger serves a useful purpose when it leads to positive action. Therefore, our response to anger must be according to Jesus's character. Justified or not, anger is never to control us. We are to be controlled by the Spirit of God. *"A person with good sense is patient, and it's to his credit that he overlooks an offense"* (Proverbs 19:11).

Day Three: Our Objects of Anger

Never go to bed mad. Stay awake and fight. —Phyllis Diller

Anger hurts because it makes us suffer.

Our objects of anger vary: parents, God, family, friends, mates, ourselves, other people, an object or obstacle, injustice, or those in authority. Whoever or whatever the object, one solution to preventing and letting go of our anger is to express it either verbally or in writing. The goal is to unload the poison of resentment from within ourselves. When we allow anger and hate to take root we become its slave. Proverbs 15:17 says, *"Better a meal of vegetables where there is love than a fattened calf with hatred."*

We Get Angry …

When others do not deal fairly with us. In 1 Samuel 25:1–34, David protected Nabal's flocks, but Nabal would not return the favor by giving David's men a share of his harvest. This made David angry, and in return, he set out to destroy Nabal. It was Abigail (Nabal's wife), who brought David to his senses when she asked him to forgive Nabal. David forgave him and brought his anger under God's control. And God ultimately dealt with Nabal.

When we are mistreated or abused. In 1 Samuel 20, Jonathon got angry over his father's treatment of David. Perhaps you can relate to Jonathan if you have a family member who is abusive or you live with an angry person. Your anger must be dealt with. It's a fact that pent up anger can cause us to mistreat others, even our own children.

Because of the sin of others. In Exodus, Moses experienced frustration and anger many times while he led the rebellious children of Israel.

Jealousy. In 1 Samuel 18:7–8, King Saul's response to the praise given David was, *"They have credited David with tens of thousands but me with only thousands."* Saul wanted to kill David because of this. We get angry when someone else is successful and happy because we are not successful or happy.

Pressure, interruption, irritation, or inconvenience in our lives. 1 Samuel 17:28–29 is another example of burning anger when David visits his brothers while Goliath is challenging their army.

When we cannot fulfill someone else's expectations or they cannot fulfill ours. Genesis 30:2 describes Jacob getting upset with his wife Rachel because she complained that he hadn't given her children. We can all point to a parent, friend, mate, perhaps even a pastor, who hurt us because they couldn't fulfill our expectations. We became angry with that person.

Having our sins exposed by others. When we sin, we don't want to be found out. If we get caught, watch out! The fury can be great. We see this in Numbers 22:21–35 when Balaam beats his donkey.

Personal pride. Pride is of the flesh, so when our pride is hurt, we become angry. In 2 Chronicles 25:10, King Amaziah sent home a group of soldiers before they could fight in a battle, and they became angry.

When someone embarrasses us. Many times, people will turn against someone and seek to hurt them because they've been humiliated and/or embarrassed. In the book of Esther, King Xerxes got angry when his wife Queen Vashti embarrassed him by refusing to be displayed to the people and nobles (1:11). He was so angry he had her replaced (2:4).

Jesus's example helps me deal with my anger. As He hung on that cross, enduring a most grotesque and humiliating form of torture, He said, *"Father, forgive them, for they do not know what they are doing" (Luke 23:34)*. As God, He could see right through to their souls. They were victims to Him.

I always remember counsel a psychology professor gave us: *hurt people, hurt people*. This advice has helped me let go of many forms of personal anger.

Verbalize Your Anger

Negative feelings cause a crushed spirit, and open us up to the schemes of Satan. God's Word tells us that anger cannot be hidden or denied—it must be addressed immediately. Bring your anger out of the darkness and into the light. One of the healthiest ways to get rid of pent up anger is to verbally express it.

Visualize in your mind going to this person and saying, "I must tell you how I feel about this situation." Write out the scenario in your journal.
Or, you may complete this letter to God. If you are angry with more than one person, write a separate letter to each person. If you are part of a group, be prepared to read one of the letters at your next meeting.

Dear God, I am angry with … for … because [person] hurt me when … and now I feel …

Day Four: Anger at Our Parents

Getting angry can sometimes be like leaping into a wonderfully responsive sports car, gunning the motor, taking off at high speed and then discovering the brakes are out of order. —Maggie Scarf

I hate my parents!

Quite often, the people who are responsible for our anger are the people we love most, our parents. Often, they aren't even aware of their actions. Angie said, "My dad says that I'm just sinning, and what I must confess and repent in order to eat normal again. My "sinning" makes him mad. He makes me mad too."

Perhaps you experienced some form of physical, sexual, emotional, and/or spiritual neglect or abuses. It's possible that your issues with food and image may have developed from this. Frequently, we turn to food and substances to meet a rational human need for love and acceptance. Please don't let anyone blame you for trying to meet your basic human needs.

Anger at Ourselves

On the other hand, maybe there is no one you are angry with except yourself. You should be! Look at what this monster has done. It's robbed you of life. Heather said, "I'm so angry with myself for wasting my life like this. I'm angry at my mind for feeding me self-loathing thoughts. But most of all, I'm angry at myself for lacking the strength to beat this." Heather has the right to feel mad and sad. Emotional eating is a *loss* of life.

Day Five: Anger at God

What has taken away your reason? What has weakened your vision that you turn against God and say all these evil things? –Eliphaz, speaking in Job 15:12-13

How do you treat God when you're angry?

Terry wrote, "I feel like God is punishing me all the time and wants me to suffer. I'm angry that I'm not worth a miracle. I've suffered long enough and have sincerely tried to change. I feel like I will never get well. Why won't God help me?"

What possible reason is there to get angry with the Almighty?

We get angry with God when we see or feel suffering. Job is a biblical person with whom we can identify with in some way. This poor man lost *everything*. His sufferings equate closely to Christ on the cross. I think we've all had a taste of the cross, of being crushed. Yet Scripture says, *"In all this, Job did not sin in what he said" (Job 2:10)*. Anger at God is never justifiable. God does not plan for bad things to happen to us. He's not the creator of evil.

We get angry with God when He doesn't conform to our ways or understanding. In Genesis 4:1–8, Cain got angry because he wanted to worship God his way. He became angry when God rejected his sacrificial offering. If other people or circumstances have hurt you, you may be angry with God because you don't understand why a God of love would allow such things to happen to you or someone you love. We all know someone who has lost a child, and we're not surprised that they would be angry with God for the loss. God understands.

We get angry with God because of His judgment. In 1 Chronicles 13:9–11, David gets angry because God kills Uzi for touching the Ark of the Covenant. In the book of Revelation, men get mad at God for His judgments upon the earth. Today, many suffering people are living out the consequences of their own sin. They're angry with God because He judged them after they broke His commandments.

We become angry with God because we want Him to judge others fairly. In Jonah 1:1–11, Jonah got mad at God because He wouldn't destroy the Ninevites, whom he hated. Think about all the people who were angry and bitter towards God for allowing the Holocaust. Why didn't God destroy Hitler before he committed all of those terrible atrocities?

What do you think the results will be if you don't release your anger to God? Ask the Holy Spirit to search your heart to see if you have any unresolved anger against God or anyone else. If He doesn't show you anything, then pray for others doing this study. Write down anything that God brings to mind.

If you're angry with God *state your case.* Tell Him what you're angry about. Use colorful language, but don't swear. God isn't hurt by your anger. But remember, as His child, He isn't responsible to answer to you.

Day Six: Grieve the Losses

A man, when he does not grieve, hardly exists. –Antonio Porsche

Grieving is a significant part of the recovery process.

Real healing began when I shifted my thinking from guilt and shame to grief and sadness. In other words, toxic emotions gave way to healthy emotions. I had lost my worth and dignity, my health, and precious time, which God highly valued. Allowing myself to be genuinely sad broke the strongholds that guilt and shame constructed. Through the enlightenment and direction of the Holy Spirit I began capturing the toxic thoughts and separated these emotions.

Some people don't feel any loss. They feel the opposite—they're discovering themselves. If that's you, then pray for your sisters who are grieving. If you begin to experience feelings of sadness you can come back. Everything you've been doing so far has been preparing you for the grief process. Maybe you're already experiencing genuine sadness in regard to your behaviors. Something as simple as setting new boundaries around food or our bodies represents a major loss. It's like losing a good friend.

Scripture says, *"It's better to go to a house of mourning than to go to a house of feasting" (Ecclesiastes 7:2)*. Grieve your losses. Grieve whatever season of life you were in when you feel you lost your way and/or your innocence. I needed to grieve my adolescence and young adulthood because I could never get it back.

Schedule Time to Grieve

What some counselors suggest, and I am one of them, is that we "schedule" processing our emotions into our daily lives. Schedule in some quality time to grieve over the losses which have resulted: relationships, experiences, job opportunities, and dreams. Begin by writing down what you feel your greatest loss has been and anyone you have held responsible for it.

Be sad. Cry. Weep. Wail alone. Grieve with other human beings. The sadness may stay over a period of days or even months. Everyone grieves differently. Don't be surprised to find that you must go through this exercise several times. This is normal as new feelings and wounds surface. You're peeling though different layers or emotions such as anger, depression, shame, guilt, and sadness.

Each loss must be acknowledged and grieved. Resist the tendency to get "stuck." This is what Satan will want you to do. This is why it's important to have at least one other safe person to talk with so you can process your feelings. If your feelings become overwhelming, consider seeing a professional counselor.

Closing Moments

Anger can be useful and valuable.

The Bible doesn't tell us we shouldn't deny conflict, but it points out it is important to handle anger properly. *"In your anger do not sin: Do not let the sun go down while you are still angry, and do not give the devil a foothold" (Ephesians 4:26-27)*. Nip it in the bud! We refuse to allow the sins of others to cause us to sin further because repressed or uncontrolled anger is dangerous.

The goal of the grief work is to achieve what we've wanted all along—peace. As long as we know what to do with our anger, peace, rather than bitterness, will come as we trust God and wait patiently. This is the hardest part, to wait patiently. Trust is the key—trust in God, the One who causes all things to work together for good. Trust is the healing balm for anger.

> *Promise to Claim:* A gentle answer turns away wrath, but a harsh word stirs up anger." (Proverbs 15:1)

Week 5

Freedom Through Forgiveness

There is a solution for the elimination of the cancer of toxic anger, for the restoration of emotional and spiritual health. It is found in *forgiveness*. The Bible says to forgive. But what do we do when confronted with the unforgivable—an act that shakes our world, often committed by someone trusted and loved?

Most of us are familiar with The Lord's Prayer:

"Forgive us our sins, for we also forgive everyone who sins against us" (Luke 11:4). Do we really mean that we want God Almighty to forgive us when we aren't willing to forgive those who hurt us? We may not even know ourselves that we're harboring bitterness and unforgiveness against someone else.

Jesus said, *"For if you forgive men when they sin against you, your heavenly Father will also forgive you. But if you do not forgive men their sins, your Father will not forgive your sins" (Matthew 6:14–15)*. This sounds serious! Dr. Charles Stanley has a good definition of forgiveness:

> "Forgiveness refers to giving up both resentment toward someone else, and the right to get even, no matter what that person has done. Unforgiveness, then, describes a deliberate refusal to let go of ill will or your right to repay the offender in some fashion; it's based on the unChristlike attitude that somebody has to pay for the hurt, a position for which there is simply no biblical justification."[15]

Forgiveness is saying, "I'm not going to hurt anymore because of what someone else did to me, even if they're not sorry." Forgiveness is a choice and a process, a process that's not all that neat and tidy. I knew if I was to grow, then I had to release the hurts of my past. This meant that I had to ask God to empower me to move forward to forgive those responsible, whether they deserved it or not. Eventually I forgave the people who hurt, teased, and rejected me.

The hardest person to forgive was myself. I hated myself because I wasted so many productive years and spent so much money catering to the monster bulimia. There were so many things I wanted back and to do over.

In each of our lives there are victims of our dependencies. I asked for my mother's forgiveness. I confessed to her that I stole money from her to support my food and laxative addiction. She forgivingly said, "What you did hasn't changed the way I love and think of you. We've all done things that we aren't proud of. There isn't anyone to judge you except God. And we know how forgiving He is." I felt the last chain and shackle fall off. It was freeing to give and receive forgiveness. Now it's your turn!

> *Note: There is 6 days this week and slightly more work because forgiveness is so critical to healing. I encourage you to put more time aside this week for this very important lesson.*

Day One: Getting Real About Forgiveness

A root of bitterness is so potent it will invade other's people's gardens, and worst of all, it will choke the grace of God in my life. I will miss what I want most.

–Paula Rinehart

Many of us have been victims of some form of abuse—emotionally, physically, or verbally abused by a family member we most likely trusted and loved. If there ever was a tragic victim, it was Tamar. A beautiful, royal princess, the daughter of King David, her life should have been a fairy tale. Instead, it became a nightmare. Her spoiled and deceitful half-brother, Amnon, raped her. Then his lust changed to hatred. Scripture says,

> *"Then Amnon hated her with intense hatred. In fact, he hated her more than he had loved her. Amnon said to her, "Get up and get out!" "No!" she said to him. "Sending me away would be a greater wrong than what you have already done to me." But he refused to listen to her. He called his personal servant and said, "Get this woman out of here and bolt the door after her""* (2 Samuel 13:15-17).

In that culture the law mandated that when a man raped an unmarried woman he had to pay a dowry, marry, and never divorce her.[16] Tamar was telling Amnon that by sending her away and not marrying her he was destroying her future. Grieving, Tamar tore her robe (a symbol of her virginity) and wept loudly. Absalom, another brother, appeared to deny Tamar her grief and discounted her emotions by saying, *"Be quiet now, my sister, he is your brother. Don't take this thing to heart"* (2 Samuel 13:20). Apparently, David was furious, but did nothing.

What happened to Tamar? Scripture says she lived in Absalom's house a ruined and desolate woman. *Ruined. Desolate.* Tamar lost hope. She had every reason to feel anger, hurt, shame, grief—even hate. Did her despair and shame surface as an addiction or as depression? Did she ever find another person to pour her wounded heart out to, or forgive those who hurt her? Did she ever find the comfort of God?

Healing begins with the understanding that God is sovereign and in control. Tamar had every reason to be angry, even hate Amnon. We all have hurts, and we all have someone in our lives that we're angry and resentful of; perhaps it's only ourselves.

The Cost of an Unforgiving Spirit

Unforgiveness is guaranteed to hinder our growth because an unforgiving spirit's an evil spirit that causes devastation. It plants roots of bitterness in our hearts. It's like pouring acid in us, a caustic substance that eats through our heart. Dorothy wrote, "My mother owes me. I lost my childhood because of her neglect and drunkenness. I hate her."

It can feel too hard to "forgive and forget" the injuries of life. God never promised any of us freedom from pain. Yet, we can begin to find happiness if we free our mind of resentment and bitterness—put the past behind and begin to see the process as empowering. Yes, forgiveness can be empowering!

When we begin living in the light, in an atmosphere of humility and honesty, we take risks. Unless humility and honesty result in forgiveness, relationships cannot be mended and strengthened. Peter recognized this and asked Jesus how he should handle these risks in Matthew 18:21–35, the parable of the unmerciful servant.

"Then Peter came to Jesus and asked, "Lord, how many times shall I forgive my brother when he sins against me? Up to seven times?" Jesus answered, "I tell you, not seven times, but seventy-seven times." Therefore, the kingdom of heaven is like a king who wanted to settle accounts with his servants. As he began the settlement, a man who owed him ten thousand talents was brought to him. Since he was not able to pay, the master ordered that he and his wife and his children and all that he had be sold to repay the debt. The servant fell on his knees before him. "Be patient with me," he begged, "and I will pay back everything."

The servant's master took pity on him, canceled the debt and let him go. But when that servant went out, he found one of his fellow servants who owed him a hundred denarii. He grabbed him and began to choke him. "Pay back what you owe me!" he demanded. His fellow servant fell to his knees and begged him, "Be patient with me, and I will pay you back." But he refused. Instead, he went off and had the man thrown into prison until he could pay the debt. When the other servants saw what had happened, they were greatly distressed and went and told their master everything that had happened.

Then the master called the servant in. "You wicked servant," he said, "I canceled all that debt of yours because you begged me to. Shouldn't you have had mercy on your fellow servant just as I had on you?" In anger his master turned him over to the jailers to be tortured, until he should pay back all he owed. "This is how my heavenly Father will treat each of you unless you forgive your brother from your heart.""

Like Dorothy and the wicked servant, you can hold that person responsible, harbor hatred, and consequently, carry feelings of anger forever. Or you can begin healing when you choose to forgive. In order to heal, we must forgive again and again—the big wrongs and the little ones. The alternative is to hold on to hatred and bitterness, which eventually will hurt all our relationships.

Author and speaker Sheila Walsh wrote,

"In my situation, as long as I was unwilling to let go and forgive, there was still a nail in my wrist, and every time I talked to someone about the situation, it cut in a little deeper."[17]

It's our responsibility, with the help of the Holy Spirit, to pull out that nail. Many people won't choose to forgive. They live unhappy lives of bitterness. If it was a parent who hurt them, they become that parent, in spite of the fact they swore they never would. Dr. Gregory Jantz wrote,

> "If the child of the past and the adult of the present are to integrate fully into the person of the future, there comes a time when both must release the hurts of the past. This doesn't mean that you forget what has been done to you, but that you forgive those responsible, whether they deserve your forgiveness or not. Forgiveness is the final destination on your healing journey. The road that lies beyond is one of health."[18]

Paul said one reason for forgiveness is to keep from being beaten by Satan. Satan knows bitterness and anger are destructive. He will exploit those emotions. God casts our sins into the depths of the sea (see Micah 7:19). We should do the same with the sins of others. In so doing, we cast Satan down with them.

Day Two: Unlock a Life of Freedom

We achieve inner health only through forgiveness—the forgiveness not only of others but also of ourselves. –Joshua Loth Liebman

I'll never forgive him as long as I live!

Many of our problems come as a result of an unforgiving attitude toward others who have offended us. I heard a story of a woman who was sexually molested frequently by her father. She became pregnant three times. One pregnancy was aborted, the second resulted in a child who died, and the third, a deformed child who lived. When she tried to tell police, her parents didn't back her up. Instead they called her a liar. At that point, she became suicidal. As a result, she never allowed anyone to touch her. Who can blame her?

Understandably, she couldn't forgive her father. What her father did makes us angry. This kind of evil makes God angry too. This is righteous, justified anger. Once this woman realized and understood that God was angry with her father the healing process began. Naturally, it took time.

Years passed, and God did miraculous things in this woman because she chose to forgive her father. She now loves being a woman, and people who knew her before say you wouldn't even recognize her. She leaned on God's Word to trust Him as the Father she never knew.

Jesus stressed the urgency of reconciliation. Paul counsels us,

"Therefore, as God's chosen people, holy and dearly loved, clothe yourselves with compassion, kindness, humility, gentleness, and patience. Bear with each other and forgive whatever grievances you may have against one another" (Colossians 3:12–13).

Won't you do the same; forgive those you harbor unforgiveness against? When you do, you'll find your relationship with God and others will become more enjoyable. People will say, "You wouldn't even recognize her now!"

Decisional and Emotional Forgiveness

Forgiveness is a process and a decision. There two concepts or types of forgiveness: *decisional* and *emotional*. Dr. Neil Anderson sums them both up in this statement: "Don't wait to forgive until you feel like forgiving. You will never get here. Feelings take time to heal after the choice to forgive is made."[19]

The decisional forgiveness process usually comes first. I choose to obey God, *"Be kind and compassionate to one another, forgiving each other, just as in Christ God forgave you" (Ephesians 4:32).* I say, "You hurt and wronged me but I choose not to hold it against you. I trust God to judge you fairly."

Decisional forgiveness is not a feeling but an act of my will to obey God. I choose not to hold this injustice against you or seek revenge. I want to put this behind me and move on. I may put a safeguard or boundary into place so this event doesn't happen again. I'm making a decision about my behavioral intentions. I also tell Satan, "I'm not giving you a foothold in my mind any longer!"

Pray. Talk to God in your own words. Reaffirm your faith and trust in Him by getting right back into his Word.

"God, as you know, I'm having difficulty forgiving [*name*]. I know I'm not following your commandment to forgive. Thank you that in your blood there is cleansing and forgiveness. However, right now, drawing on your strength, I'm making a decision to forgive [*name*]. I take [*name*] off my hook and place [*name*] on your hook. I thank and praise you for forgiving me, and being patient and understanding."

The second type, *emotional forgiveness*, is the process of replacing negative emotions with positive emotions. With decisional forgiveness, I choose to forgive you, but I cannot manage my negative emotions. I continue to hang onto bitterness, anger, hatred, and fear. We often need the help of a professional counselor or pastor, along with the support of friends.

Decisional forgiveness takes place instantaneously, while emotional forgiveness can be a recovery process. It may take years to heal depending on the depth of the wound. Or it might happen quickly. It's the process of emotionally releasing and forgiving, perhaps time and again. And let us not forget, forgiving and escaping consequences are not synonymous.

Forgiveness is a choice—our choice alone. It's a gift from God to the forgiver. It's also a gift from the forgiver to the person who doesn't deserve this gift. It's the hardest call of a Christian. Every day you must make the *decision* to forgive. Every day you must take your *emotions* to God.

Day Three: What Forgiveness is Not

Only a free person can choose to live with an uneven score. –Lewis Smedes

Kerri said, "He did horrible, abusive things to me. He thinks he's justified and shows no remorse. He doesn't deserve forgiveness!"

The Bible counsels us to *"make every effort to do what leads to peace and to mutual edification" (Romans 14:19)*. But if your addiction is the result of a traumatic or tragic event, forgiveness will most likely be difficult. It's normal to feel that forgiveness is impossible, but it's necessary if you want victory. With God, it is possible.

It's common to want the person who has hurt us to show remorse or confess their guilt before we forgive them. Often, this never happens. Some argue that since Christ forgives us, we should not only forgive others, but fully relinquish them from the consequences of their actions. I don't believe this is what God intends. (I'll be sharing Scripture to support this.)

We must mentally separate the act of forgiveness and the act of reuniting. They are not the same. Forgiving the person is about changing us, not the offender. If they sincerely repent and ask for forgiveness, and give ample evidence of changed behavior, then a reunion *may* be possible.

What God desires is a broken spirit and repentant heart (Psalm 51:17). To freely forgive is the biblically correct position. But it's an altogether different matter to suggest that once forgiven, a person is free from any consequences. Let's look at what forgiveness does *not* do.

Forgiveness Does Not Let the Person off the Hook

Often an offender's actions destroy lives. This doesn't mean you don't hold the person accountable. God does: *"I, the LORD, search all hearts and examine secret motives. I give all people their due rewards, according to what their actions deserve"* *(Jeremiah 17:10)*. Forgiveness involves mercy and grace, but it also involves accountability.

God's love is two-sided—mercy and judgment—which deals with accountability. Many women struggle with this because it means setting boundaries and following through with consequences. Part of this process is coming to understand that God sets consequences. So, we must too.

In 2 Samuel 11 and 12 we meet King David and are given a recap of his disturbing escapades. Considered a man after God's own heart, he committed adultery and then murdered a man in a final effort to cover his own sin. He refused to admit what he'd done. David's adultery with Bathsheba was a sin of passion, a sin of the moment which overtook him. But having Bathsheba's husband, Uriah, killed was premeditated, deliberate, and a disgrace against God.

Scripture says the *"LORD considered David's actions evil"* *(2 Samuel 11:27, GW)*. Other versions say the thing David had done displeased God. Notice God is angry with David's actions, not David, His child.

At this point in time Bathsheba and David were about to have a baby. God sent in the prophet Nathan to confront the guilty king about his actions. By telling a story about someone else's crime, Nathan prepared David for dealing with his own sins. David saw the truth and confessed.

God judged David's sins and he paid dearly for his deceit for the rest of his lifetime. *"Because you despised me and took the wife of Uriah the Hittite to be your own. … Out of your own household I am going to bring calamity upon you" (2 Samuel 10-11).*

These verses came true. The consequences were irreversible. *Sin which has been forgiven and forgotten by God may still leave human scars.*

We know David truly repented because he wrote Psalm 51 during this event. He knew he had to be cleansed by God. We see a changed man, a man with a genuine contrite heart. Despite David's actions, God continued to use him. In fact, his virtues were found worthy enough to generate from his seed the forthcoming Messiah.

Forgiveness Does Not Excuse, Condone, Deny, Minimize, or Justify the Behavior

When my sister-in-law stole from me she made me mad. After she apologized I said, "That's okay," even though it wasn't alright. When someone apologizes, often the other person answers, "That's okay," because she has been told to "forgive and forget." Yet, she still hurts and is distrustful.

Forgiveness is *not* saying, "It's not a big deal." If it truly is no big deal, then there's nothing to forgive. If it's a real offense against you, God's daughter, it is a big deal—so big that Jesus Christ died for it.

Many offenders want you to take responsibility for their behavior. If you're ever confused about whom the victim is, or if you find yourself apologizing for how you caused the person to offend you or others, you're playing into the devil's hands. However, we must be honest about the part we played in the situation. For example, if I leave money in plain sight knowing my sister is a kleptomaniac, then, I have facilitated the theft.

When God forgives our sin He's not saying our past behavior is disregarded. What if somebody has a history of abusing children? Although they experience God's forgiveness, the laws of our land demand they be held criminally responsible for their crime. Even after they've served their sentence, prudence still dictates the person not volunteer in children's ministry.

Forgiveness Does Not Forget

There are two words which shouldn't be associated with forgiveness: *forgive* and *forget*. The fact is, we don't forget. Brain studies reveal whatever is important to us is stashed away in our long-term memory.[20] Paul told the Philippians, *"I forget what is behind, and I struggle for what is ahead." (Philippians 3:13-14)*. The biblical word *forget* in this context does not mean "put out of one's mind." It has the meaning of letting go. It means we're not going to allow the experiences of the past to dominate our future and prevent us from becoming all God has purposed.

There are memories we cannot put out of our minds. But we choose not to allow them to dictate our attitudes and behavior in the future, even toward those who may be responsible for those memories.

Furthermore, if someone is taught to be a "good Christian" and to forgive and forget, the offender, and others involved, may get the message this behavior is acceptable. Whether we've forgiven the person depends not on whether we remember the incident, but rather it depends on our attitude. We know we've truly forgiven when we're no longer controlled by the pain, or no longer wish the person dead. We still remember what happened, but that memory no longer has power over our thinking and behavior.

Forgiveness Does Not Mean Reconciliation

People are generally reluctant to forgive because they don't understand the difference between forgiveness and trust. Forgiveness is not letting go of the past, nor is it an expectation of a future relationship with the person. It doesn't mean letting the offender back into your life. Forgiveness is your gift. If someone continues to hurt you, God commands you to forgive them now. But you're not commanded to trust them. They must prove they've changed over time. If a relationship with any person is not healthy, it's appropriate to distance yourself. Jesus always withdrew from a situation if it was about to become violent or unhealthy (with the exception of the crucifixion).

Forgiveness Does Not Wait for an Apology

Some say, "I'll forgive her as soon as she says she's sorry." The truth is some people will never apologize. There are people who will continue in their destructive, rebellious, and foolish behavior. Others will be stubborn and never confess or admit their sin. Some will move away, and others will die before they ever repent. We choose to forgive them because we know this is God's desire.

Writing a Forgiveness List

Whose forgiveness might you need the most: another person or God or yourself? Begin the process by writing a forgiveness list of everyone *you have hurt*. With God's help, think again. Have you forgotten or over-looked anyone? Reject the idea you've hurt no one. This is a test of humility. Example:

Person	Relationship	Nature of Harm	The Sin	Effect on Others	Effect on Me	Act Of Forgiveness
John	husband	angry insults	dishonest, anger	fear, anger	guilt, shame	
Mary	co-worker	stole her snacks	grandiosity	anger, distrust	guilt, shame	

Do not fill in the "Act of Forgiveness" column yet. You will come back to it. Consider each person carefully and prayerfully. Look at each relationship and consider how you hurt the person. Be as thorough as possible. For example, "I have stolen money from my husband to buy food. The amount of money that I've spent on food could have been used for a down payment on a house by now; I have lied to my counselor Jennie and my family about the severity and frequency of my bingeing and purging."

Day Four: Restoring Relationships

To err is human, to forgive divine. –Alexander Pope

We all have a past, a not so wonderful past.

Our painful pasts may be a consequence of our own bad choices and self-inflicted wounds. Often however, the heartache has been caused by others in the form of betrayal, unfaithfulness, deceit, accusation, broken trust, or slander. It is impossible to live out God's plan for our future when we live in the pain of the past.

In Genesis 37, we meet Joseph, Jacob's son who gives us a great example of this principle. Joseph was Jacob's favorite son, and all the other brothers knew it. "They hated him and could not speak a kind word to him." We follow Joseph through a series of near-tragic events brought about at the hands of his brothers and others. Genesis 31–34 says,

> *"Come now, let's kill him and throw him into one of these cisterns and say that a ferocious animal devoured him." Then his brothers sold him to a caravan of Ishmaelite slave traders heading for Egypt. Worst yet, the brothers got Joseph's robe, slaughtered a goat, and dipped the robe in the blood. They took the ornamented robe back to their father and said, "We found this. Examine it to see whether it's your son's robe." He recognized it and said, "It's my son's robe! Some ferocious animal has devoured him. Joseph has surely been torn to pieces."*

The brothers and their grieving father, Jacob, never expected to see Joseph again. However, God had a different plan. Contrary to his brother's expectations, Joseph did very well in Egypt. He was given a prominent position in the house of Potiphar. He proved to be reliable, innovative, and hardworking. Then Potiphar's wife wanted to bed Joseph, but he refused to give into temptation. She cried rape and Joseph was thrown into prison (Genesis 39:17, TLB).

If I were Joseph, I would have been angry and heartbroken by my brother's betrayal, at Potiphar's wife for crying rape, and at the Lord for allowing my incarceration, when all I was doing was the honorable thing. Was Joseph angry? Scripture is silent, but those years had to be long and dark. I can almost hear him say, *Lord, I chose to honor you. Why didn't you come to my defense?* God was with Joseph. Genesis 39:20–23 says,

"Joseph's master took him and put him in prison, the place where the king's prisoners were confined. But while Joseph was there in the prison, the Lord was with him; he showed him kindness and granted him favor in the eyes of the prison warden. So the warden put Joseph in charge of all those held in the prison, and he was made responsible for all that was done there. The warden paid no attention to anything under Joseph's care, because the Lord was with Joseph and gave him success in whatever he did."

We're tempted to think that when God is with us, everything will work out perfectly. This isn't the case. What is important is how we handle our situation. We see that no matter what happened to Joseph, he found favor with God because of how he lived. He accepted the death of his dreams and waited to fulfill God's plan for his life.

Joseph had no idea that in a few years he'd be taken out of jail to interpret a dream for Pharaoh and then put in charge of Egypt. He had no idea that all the years in prison were preparing him for the rest of his life. God knew. Shift to God's perspective as a parent. I believe He deliberately pulled back to allow Joseph's faith to mature.

Joseph is then given the opportunity to reveal himself to his brothers. He tests them to determine if they've developed any character since they abandoned him. Then Joseph said to his brothers,

""Come close to me." When they had done so, he said, "I am your brother Joseph, the one you sold into Egypt! And now, do not be distressed and do not be angry with yourselves for selling me here, because it was to save lives that God sent me ahead of you. For two years now there has been famine in the land, and for the next five years there will not be plowing and reaping. But God sent me ahead of you to preserve for you a remnant on earth and to save your lives by a great deliverance" (Genesis 45: 4–7).

The tables were turned. The brothers were devastated. Egypt was the only place with grain, and Joseph had charge over distributing it. If I were Joseph, I'd be thinking, *Why should I help them? They tried to kill me!* His brothers threw themselves down before him. "We are your slaves," they said. But Joseph said to them,

"Don't be afraid. Am I in the place of God? You intended to harm me, but God intended it for good to accomplish what is now being done, the saving of many lives" (Genesis 50:20–21).

Joseph didn't blame his brothers; he provided for them. The same lips that once begged his brothers to stop and trembled with fear, now spoke with unwavering confidence in God's plan. Joseph's faith in God's character enabled him to forgive his brothers. *That's why we can be so sure that every detail in our lives of love for God is worked into something good"* (Romans 8:28, MSG)—rejection in one's childhood, alcoholic parents, a cheating husband, or illness.

No matter what life has in store for us, *God can turn anything into a blessing*. Yes, anything! So, let go of the past. Look towards the future and let God turn your life around.

Day Five: Mending Fences

Being unwilling to forgive means that we hold everyone around us to a standard of perfection—something that we ourselves will never achieve."

–Gary L. Thomas, Authentic Faith

How do you feel about a heart transplant?

Before starting this study, many of us blamed others for the turmoil in our lives. Some of us held God responsible. It's time to release the need to blame others and accept full responsibility for our own lives. This means letting go of that hard-heartedness, one of the greatest blocks to our ability to give and receive love. We ask for forgiveness which means restoring personal relationships—mending fences.

When I was a kid, I fought all the time with my brothers. We constantly tattled and blamed each other, which is pretty normal. Eventually, we grew up. Now, we're being asked to grow up and do what spiritually mature people do—take responsibility for our actions without consideration for hurts and wrongs done to us by others.

Our willingness to mend the fences in our lives gives us an opportunity to love one another and experience God living in us. It increases our self-esteem. It may or may not benefit the other person; he or she may not be willing to put matters aside. That doesn't matter. *We will heal.*

Forgiving Those Who Have Hurt Us

John Chrysostom said, *"Nothing causes us to so nearly resemble God as the forgiveness of injuries."* Receiving the gift of God's love and forgiveness, then *giving it to others freely* assures us of an abundant life. This is another secret to healing!

Jesus said, *"Do not judge, and you will not be judged. Do not condemn, and you will not be condemned. Forgive, and you will be forgiven. Give, and it will be given to you"* *(Luke 6:37–38).* Hate binds. Love frees. We forgive those who have hurt us no matter what they've done so *we can be free.* Jesus also reminds us,

> *"Why do you look at the speck of sawdust in your brother's eye and pay no attention to the plank in your own eye? How can you say to your brother, 'Let me take the speck out of your eye,' when all the time there is a plank in your own eye?"* *(Matthew 7:3–4)*

Psalm 66:18 says sin, including unresolved conflict, blocks our fellowship with God and keeps our prayers from being answered (and makes us miserable). When we choose to forgive, we can finally let go of the past and begin anew.

Forgiving and Honoring a Parent

Are you harboring unforgiveness toward a parent?

I could always find reasons to blame my parents for my past, but as God healed my heart I realized they did the best they could with what they were given. Some of us may lack the ability to speak back to our parents, or function as an adult in their presence. Some of us have difficulties setting boundaries due to underlying issues that haven't been identified yet.

Perhaps one of your parents is, or has been, physically, emotionally, or verbally abusive to you (and may no longer be part of your life). Forgiving and honoring a parent doesn't mean we allow them to continue to hurt us; that we become doormats for others to wipe their feet on as they enter in and walk on our hearts. At some point, we must set a boundary.

To honor our parent may look like this: I acknowledge my parent's sin (for example, verbal abuse). I forgive the wrong, which may be difficult. It is still necessary for my emotional freedom and my relationship with Jesus. Without getting angry, I tell my parent I won't be spoken to in this manner. My parent must comply and choose to speak respectfully to me or I will remove myself from the situation. I don't publicly demean or trash my parent. I'm not however, obligated to maintain a relationship with anyone who does not treat me as I should be treated, as a child of God. I can close the relational door. I don't want to lock it as my parent's heart may change, thereby creating an opportunity for the relationship to be restored.

Take a deep breath and tell God you're ready to forgive your parent for not being the person you wanted him or her to be.

Writing a Forgiveness Letter

Forgiveness does not deny we hurt, possibly even hate. It is not promising to never talk about the wrongdoing or hurt feelings. Most psychologists and pastors recommend dealing with childhood issues, if possible. This may mean re-establishing contact with parents. Obviously, you cannot if a parent is dead or antagonistic. Discussing the past may provide some parents a much-needed emotional release. But don't be surprised, some will deny their actions.

Consider writing a letter about the hurt. Writing a letter about the things this person did can bring the hurt to the light. Open the door by thanking this person for the things they did right in your relationship—even if it's only a few things. Then pray about whether you should speak to this person or send a letter.

Begin the process by writing a letter in your journal to the person you need to forgive for hurting you, even if it's yourself. Tell them how you feel and what you regret. Ask the Holy Spirit to release them from your judgment. Or you can write out a statement of forgiveness: "Dear God, I forgive [*name*] for … [*specific action*]."

If you are part of a group, be prepared to read one of your letters at your next meeting.

Day Six: Forgiveness in Action

Real success is measured by the courage it takes to do and say what needs to be done or said. –Paula Rinehart, Strong Women, Soft Hearts

Damare, a small Sudanese boy, was taken as a slave and forced to tend camels after radical Muslims attacked his village. One day, Damare, who had been raised in a Christian home, snuck away to attend a church service. When he returned, his Muslim master was waiting for him. He accused Damare of committing a deadly act, "meeting with infidels." He dragged Damare into a field. He nailed his feet and knees into a large board while the boy cried out in agony. Miraculously rescued, Damare said he chose to forgive because "Jesus was nailed and forgave."[21]

What bold faith from a simple Sudanese boy! This story brought tears to my eyes as I thought of all the petty grievances I imagined so horrible. Like Damare, we're asked to complete the forgiveness process.

Have you ever noticed when you put your garbage can out week after week, there's always that gunk stuck on the bottom that never gets discarded. It stays stuck on the bottom until you wash it out with soap and water. That's what we're doing, washing out that gunk.

Don't be scared off. The qualities we need to wash out the gunk are available from God. He can give us the judgment and careful sense of timing, courage, and stamina we need.

Don't expect to suddenly feel love for this person, especially if the offense was great. Forgiving and making amends doesn't mean that what happened to you was okay or that you let this person back into your life again. You're lining up your will with God's will in simple obedience.

The Rebuilding Process

Natural disasters are prevalent and always gripping news. What happens to these devastated areas after the news cameras go away? We don't see the hard work of rebuilding that takes place after the disaster. This is what we're doing; starting the rebuilding process that takes place after our hurricane blows through. It's a painfully humbling process, but very rewarding.

Remember, our forgiveness doesn't depend on the other person. All we can do is the right thing. How they react to our effort is a matter between them and God. If we caused anguish, then we ask ourselves how we best can make reparation (repair the damage). *Some kind of reparation is required,* even if we cannot completely restore the damage.

There are seven practical biblical steps to restoring and rebuilding a relationship:

1. *Pray.* Take your problem to God and tell Him exactly how you feel. We often find either God changes our heart, or He changes the other person's. God promises, "I will give them an undivided heart and put a new spirit in them; I will remove from them their heart of stone and give them a heart of flesh" (Ezekiel 11:19).

2. *Take the lead.* It doesn't matter whether we're the offender or the offended; God expects us to make the first move. Jesus commanded it even take priority over group worship. Matthew 5:23–24 tells us not to procrastinate or make excuses, as it makes matters worse. In conflict, time heals nothing; it only causes hurts to fester.

3. *Confess your part of the conflict.* If we're serious about restoring a relationship, we begin by admitting our own mistakes (sin). We ask God to show us how much of the problem is our fault. *Father, am I being unrealistic, insensitive, or too sensitive?* Honestly own up. We should also ask an unbiased person to help evaluate our actions before meeting with the person.

4. *Be sympathetic.* We shouldn't try to talk the person out of how they feel. Just listen and let them unload. Then you say, "I value your opinion. I care about our relationship."

5. *Attack the problem, not the person.* In resolving conflict, *how* we say something, along with our body language, is as important as *what* we say (see Proverbs 16:21). Avoid using harmful or hurtful words. We are never persuasive when we are abrasive.

6. *Cooperate.* We should do everything possible to live in peace with everybody. Jesus said, *"Blessed are the peacemakers, for they will be called sons of God"* (Matthew 5:9).

7. *Reconciliation, not resolution.* Not everyone will agree about everything. Reconciliation focuses on the relationship, while resolution focuses on the problem. We can agree to disagree. This doesn't mean we give up finding a solution.

The authors of *Love Hunger* wrote, "Realize that this process of repairing relationships is one-sided and one-directional. That means it's not contingent on the other person's returning the apology; it's not necessarily reciprocal."[22]

In choosing *not* to takes steps towards restoration, our only reason must be that it would result in harm to another person. Forgiveness related to adultery, crimes, or acts that might result in some kind of loss, such as being fired from a job, has the potential to harm others.

Forgiveness is a choice, a choice to obey God, regardless of our emotions. The good news is mending these broken fences leads to peace of mind and a stronger relationship with God.

Get Out Your Forgiveness List

In your column "Act of Forgiveness," describe the amend you intend to make to each person on the list. Pause right now and talk to God about these people. Pray about how you intend to make the necessary act of forgiveness.

Go down the list person by person, and approach each person with gentleness, sensitivity, and understanding. God will help you know how best to make contact (in person or by phone or letter), and the right time.

Ask yourself, "Am I willing to endure whatever consequences are necessary to complete the forgiveness process?" If the answer is no, continue to pray and keeping praying until your mind changes.

Closing Moments

Forgiveness is a choice.

No doubt you've seen your perceptions about anger and forgiveness change. The transformation in us and others that forgiveness provides is simply amazing. Here is proof: A young man was sentenced to seven years in prison for a heinous crime. His family was extremely ashamed and angry with him. Years later, when he was released he wanted to go home and be reunited. He wrote his family telling them his wishes.

He said, "I know I have hurt you and you are very angry with me. You have every right to be. I have suffered, too, and am remorseful. Please forgive me. I want to come home. If you forgive me, tie a white ribbon on the big maple tree in the pasture. Then I'll know I'm forgiven and can come home."

As the train neared his family's property, he couldn't bear to see if the white ribbon hung on the tree. He said to the man sitting next to him, "Sir, we're coming up on my family's farm. There's a big maple tree in the pasture. Is there a white ribbon hung on it?"

The passenger said, "No, there isn't one white ribbon." He paused. . . . "There are dozens of white ribbons in all the trees. In fact, there are white ribbons all over—on the clothesline, the fences, and the front porch." The young man began sobbing, "I've been forgiven! I'm home!"

Forgiveness heals the hole in our heart, the woundedness of our soul, unpleasant memories, seething rage, resentment, and the ferocity of hate. *Jesus forgave.* We have all suffered at the hands of another person, but none of us can say we've ever been crucified. Jesus underwent a horrific torture and humiliation for *our sin.* Sinless, He did nothing to deserve crucifixion. If Jesus can forgive those who tormented, tortured, and crucified Him, can you forgive those who tormented and tortured you?

When we clearly see how much we've been forgiven by God, it's easier to forgive others. To forgive is to obey God and say, "God, I love you, and I am willing to deny myself and desires."

Promise to Claim: For he has rescued us from the kingdom of darkness and transferred us into the Kingdom of his dear Son, who purchased our freedom and forgave our sins. (Colossians 1:13-14, NLT)

Week 6

Choosing Self-Discovery Over Control

Manipulating food and our image is about control.

As I reflect on my life there are three threads that run through every chapter and each season—shame, addiction, and the need to be in control. Perhaps the deepest need human beings have is for control. We can be addicted to it. Tamara wrote,

"I am a control freak probably because so many things in my life are outside of my control. The one thing I can control is my body, my weight, and what I put into it. I'm addicted to food, and bingeing is my way of acting out, escaping uncomfortable feelings, and saying I hate my life. Purging is control too. It's like being God and evading responsibility. I can rebel, and the rules don't apply to me."

Growing up, our family moved often, and with each new school I started, I met with rejection. I was always told what to do and failed numerous times. In my mind, that meant I lost control. I took to controlling the only thing I could—my own body. As a bulimic, I could ingest thousands of calories and not gain a pound. What a powerful feeling—a high, to eat whatever I wanted, when I wanted, without suffering the consequences of getting fat!

We develop issues of control in order to protect ourselves from pain due to a variety of family and sociocultural influences. If you were abused in any form, constantly rejected, or had a controlling parent, you probably felt unable to stop what was happening, so you turned to a substance or activity to deaden the pain. You think you're in complete control, but you aren't. When we feel we've lost control, we experience a powerful and uncomfortable tension. Food and/or body sculpting is one way we choose to take total charge of our bodies—all in an attempt to cope and gain some semblance of management over our lives. However, this is a false sense of control.

Our compulsive behaviors are not related to food or our behaviors, but about taking control of the actions and trying to manage the associated pain. Turning to food is only a temporary fix (Satan's stronghold) that seeks to hide the truth—the truth about the source of the pain. On the other hand, being out of control can be a good thing! It often forces us to surrender.

Healing begins with the understanding that God is sovereign and in control of our lives. Ask yourself, "Do I *really* believe God? Do I *really* trust him for my future?" We have the assurance we're not controlled by our compulsions and sinful behavior, but by the Spirit of God (Romans 8:9).

Day One Helplessness

When a controller has the sense of life being out of control, he or she reacts with an even stronger need to 'get things under control'. . . usually with the negative result of alienating the people who matter the most. –J. Keith Miller

Help has to come from a power greater than us.

Vulnerability is often equated with powerlessness or weakness. Yet vulnerability and risk is what Jesus modeled. Amy writes, "My life has become unmanageable because I need to control my food intake in a vain attempt to control how I look and as a way to feel accepted and good enough. I have no control over food because my food obsession has taken over my life, and therefore, it controls me. I know it's deception."

Satan has convinced us that we're in control of our own lives. The Bible tells us we should be careful who we listen to and choose our role models carefully, *"For Satan himself masquerades as an angel of light"* (2 Corinthians 11:14). By accepting our powerlessness and unmanageability, we are accepting that we cannot take back our life alone.

Control is also a direct response to our fear, anger, family, and sense of helplessness. It happens when we feel overwhelmed or lose trust—trust in God, the world, or ourselves. Many ask, "Can the person being controlled by food really be healed?" Dr. Gregory Jantz says,

> "Yes! There is something amazing that occurs when past hurts are resolved, and the substitute of food is no longer needed ... They take back [healthy] control over their lives that they've given over to food."[23]

We can turn this ship around by learning to have faith in God, in ourselves, and in healthy relationships. This is healing. The real breakthrough for Amy came when she finally saw how the issue of control over food and her body had dominated her life. She also realized she sought power over every situation and person. When she released her burdens to God, a huge weight was lifted off her and the transformation process began. Over time, balance and stability were restored to her life.

Take the risk and begin to release control. Give the reigns to God because *"If God is for us, who can be against us"* (Romans 8:31).

⁂

We don't know what God has in store for us. We're fearful it may be too difficult or uncomfortable, or we won't be able to measure up. There is something to be said, literally, about letting God manage our lives. Meditate on these two passages:

> *"Trust in the Lord with all your heart and lean not on your own understanding; in all your ways acknowledge him, and he will make your paths straight. Do not be wise in your own eyes; fear the Lord and shun evil. This will bring health to your body and nourishment to your bones"* (Proverbs 3:5–8).

> *"He reached down from on high and took hold of me; he drew me out of deep waters. He rescued me from my powerful enemy, from my foes, who were too strong for me. They confronted me in the day of my disaster, but the Lord was my support. He brought me out into a spacious place; he rescued me because he delighted in me"* (Psalm 18:16–19).

What beautiful promises! This healing journey may seem overwhelming, but God will give you the strength to do this.

Day Two: The Answer

When we kept our sin silent, we withdrew from God. We saw Him as an enemy. We took steps to avoid His presence. But our confession of faults alters our perception. God is no longer a foe, but a friend. We are at peace with Him. Jesus was crushed for the evil we did. The punishment, which made us well, was given to Him. He accepted the shame. He leads us into the presence of God.

–Max Lucado

God alone accomplishes our surrender.

You may be thinking, *Absolute surrender implies too much. I've bore so much pain. There's too much of my self-will remaining. I can't entirely give it up. It will cause too much agony.*

God does not ask you to surrender in your strength or by the power of your will. Look at Abraham and Moses in the Old Testament. God didn't need Abraham to pull off His plan. He didn't need Moses either. He chose Abraham. He chose Moses. Do you think that it was Abraham himself, apart from God, who had such faith, such obedience, and such devotion? No. God raised him up and prepared him as an instrument for His glory.

God told Moses to tell Pharaoh, *"I have raised you up [spared you] for this very purpose, that I might show you my power and that my name might be proclaimed in all the earth"* *(Exodus 9:16)*. And God chose me—an ordinary self-willed girl who made a lot of bad destructive choices.

If there is anything holding you back, or any sacrifice you're afraid of making, come to God now and let Him prove how gracious He is. God offers to work surrender in you. Pray, "Father, make me willing."

Up to now, believing in God did not always mean we accepted His power. As Christians, we know about God but do not necessarily invite Him into our lives. Proverbs 16:3 counsels us to commit to God everything we do and our plans will succeed. He prepares us by placing trust and faith in our hearts. This is hard if we've been let down time after time. It's easy to forget that God has a plan when we only focus on ourselves. Our focus must change.

Turbulent waters are ahead on the road to healing. God knows that. Second Corinthians 3:5 says our competence comes from God. If we trust Him, He will lead us out of the pit when we break out of denial and recognize the dysfunction in our lives. Faith isn't earned or intellectualized. Faith is a precious gift from God. *It isn't an option. Faith is a must.*

Focus on the Outcome

As Christians, we believe Jesus is God—the One who delivers us from sin and illness and destructive behavior. We have faith that He says who He is, and He, therefore, has the right to manage our lives. Jesus was incredible. In the midst of His suffering and shame, He kept focused.

> *Let us fix our eyes on Jesus, the author and perfecter of our faith, who for the joy set before him endured the cross, scorning its shame . . . (Hebrews 12:2).*

There are four messages for us in this one verse:

1—To *fix* means "to trust." Jesus said He'd send the Holy Spirit in His name to teach us and remind us of all He has said (John 14:26). *Jesus is the answer.* Set your mind and heart on Jesus who, *for you*, has defeated shame, fear, and guilt. He won't let you down. He'll always be there to help you through. Fixing our eyes on Jesus will make it easier to take our thoughts captive. Then we're not so tempted to focus on our personal problems.

2—Looking up to Jesus describes an attitude of faith, not just an act. The word *author* in Greek means "one who takes the lead." The fact that Jesus prayed is evidence He lived by faith. We follow His lead.

3—What is so joyous about being crucified? This isn't what the verse is saying. "For the joy set before him . . ." means Jesus fast-forwarded to the salvation plan and eternity. He knew He'd come out of the tomb alive in three days. He knew He'd be exalted to heaven in glory. He knew one day He'd come back for us. He was encouraged.

Jesus focused on the end result rather than the painful process. Right now, many of us are losing the battle. All we can think about is stopping the pain, stopping the behavior *today*. We're being asked to follow His lead and look ahead in faith.

The heroes of faith listed in the book of Hebrews, Chapter 11, lived for the future. This is what enabled them to endure. The author emphasized the importance of future hope. When you're in a difficult place, fast-forward and in faith anticipate the great work God is going to do. Don't ask "why," ask "what."

4—Jesus "scorned" (despised) the shame of the cross. Before the crucifixion, He underwent a merciless beating, a public mocking meant to inflict maximum pain and humiliation. The enemy tried to keep Jesus down by the weight of shame, but he lost that battle. Jesus had no shame. It was our shame He suffered on the cross, and then buried once and for all. *The burden of shame is not yours to bear any longer!*

As your battle to reclaim your life moves ahead, focus on Jesus and the ultimate outcome. You can have peace and strength—the kind that comes from focusing on His will.

Day Three: Radical Acceptance

Control masquerades as strength, but it's really not. It's more like teeth-gritting determination, or white-knuckled fear with an edge to it. –Paula Rinehart

Progress comes at the cost of leaving the old behind.

Healing requires us to understand our past. It can clarify the present and point the way to the future, but it never asks us to live or dwell in it. As much as we work to be in control of what happens to us and what we do to our bodies, the truth is we are out of balance and need a genuine solution. God wants us to move on with our renewed lives. Now, we come to acceptance (which is actually a stage of grief).

Acceptance is a key to healing. I'm not talking about winning the approval of man, but submitting to our Lord. The opposite of denial is acceptance—*radical acceptance.* The first step is to accept the sovereignty of God. God is totally and completely in charge—period. Many people pray the prayer of Reinhold Niebuhr: "God, grant me the serenity to accept the things I cannot change, courage to change the things I can, and wisdom to know the difference."[24]

Dr. Gregory Jantz, founder and CEO of The Center for Counseling & Health Resources in Edmonds Washington, found in his professional experience that regaining control of our lives comes down to acceptance. He advises:[25]

Accept what is. Could-have, should-have, and would-have are dreadful companions. A clear course must be determined from where you actually are, not where you wanted to be, thought you should be, or wish you weren't. Acceptance is the point at which you stop moving *from* something and start moving *toward* something. Acceptance designates a starting point and is often the beginning of positive change.

Accept what has happened to you in the past—you cannot go back and rewrite history. The only power is in writing your future story.

Accept how the past has shaped you—this means both the negative and positive ways you have been shaped, trusting God to use all that raw material for your good as He promised (Romans 8:28).

Accept how you have responded to your past—acceptance leads to responsibility. Your past is not only a product of what others have done to you, it's also a product of what you've done to yourself. When you are ready to take responsibility for your own life choices, you force fear to move aside so you can move forward.

Accept that you need to change—acceptance should be the change agent creating the energy you need to chart a new course. Fear tells you to maintain the status quo on the off-chance it might work. This is Albert Einstein's definition of insanity—to continue the same behavior while expecting different results.

Love yourself enough to say "no." The ability to discern what you should say yes and no to gives you back a measure of control. True self-love is not carte blanche to do whatever you want. On the contrary, true self-love allows you to deny yourself.

If we fail to accept God's truths, to accept ourselves just the way we are, and fail to live in obedience, then we fall short. Paul never allowed his sins or unattractive appearance and speech to keep him from growing and bearing fruit for Jesus. Paul accepted God's grace and could say, *"Whatever I am now is all because God poured out such kindness and grace upon me"* (1 Corinthians 15:10). We can be free of this nasty obsession if we accept His grace and let Him do the rest.

Ask God to show you if you are failing in any of these areas. Write in your journal what God shows you and what you must do about it.

Accepting Our Circumstances

Can you look back on your God-given life and say, "It needed to be this way"? If you're still regretting or fighting with your past, then you haven't reached radical acceptance.

Why do some people seem to handle trauma, disasters, and addiction without difficulty? They probably asked God to help them accept and understand uncontrollable circumstances. Acceptance means accepting and enduring *all* circumstances, even the disastrous ones. It means preparing our hearts and minds to accept the truth and consequences of our behaviors, no matter how unpleasant. It's our relationship with God that can help us be willing to bear and grow from experiences which seem impossible to cope with. Paul lived with a "thorn." Whatever plagued him was a painful, ongoing trial. Yet he said,

> *Since I know it's all for Christ's good, I am quite happy about 'the thorn,' and about insults and hardships, persecutions and difficulties; for when I am weak, then I am strong—the less I have, the more I depend on him* (2 Corinthians 12:10, TLB).

When I'm worrying over some circumstance, I seek comfort in Paul's words. When I'm the weakest and most desperate, God works my circumstance, or myself, into something good. Our success comes through our reliance and obedience on God to direct us. When we see that what we went through has molded us to be the women we are today, then we're on the road to peace.

Will you shut God out or let His power fill your thorn-formed wound? God longs for us to give our wounds to Him. Talk to Him about your struggles. Ask for His help in letting go so you can let Him take over.

Day Four: Personal Examination

A smooth sea never made a skilled mariner. –English Proverb

The "Seven Deadly Sins" pretty much covers it.

Throughout history, only seven sins have earned the right to be called "deadly:" *pride, greed, lust, envy, gluttony, anger* and *sloth*.[26] Each one is extremely dangerous because each deceives and wreaks destruction. When we repeatedly sin, it causes us to fall into bondage where, without supernatural help, we cannot break free. Sin interferes with the work of God and robs us of all God longs to give us.

Pride refers to things that satisfy a person's inner longing for value or esteem. It is an excessive belief in one's own abilities, like self-importance. It has been called the sin from which all others arise, such as selfishness, criticism, insensitivity, self-justification, narcissism, and vanity.

Envy, or jealousy, is the desire for others' traits, status, abilities, things, or situations. It can also be called self-pity and self-condemnation.

Gluttony is an inordinate desire to consume or have (as in hoarding) more than one person requires.

Lust is anything that someone uses to satisfy desires of the flesh, such as an inordinate craving for the pleasures of the body or an insatiable desire for food or chemical substances.

Anger is manifested in the individual who rejects love and opts instead for fury, hate, wrath, or bitterness.

Greed, or covetousness, is the desire for material wealth and/or personal gain.

Sloth is the avoidance of physical or spiritual work, such as laziness and procrastination.

Double-O-U-C-H! *Everyone* has a propensity toward the seven deadly sins. Each sin is a fiery dart, or missile, that Satan fires on a daily basis to keep us from believing in Jesus. His objective is to entice us to disregard God's boundaries. *The Message* paraphrase of John 3:20-21 says,

> *"Everyone who makes a practice of doing evil, addicted to denial and illusion, hates God-light and won't come near it, fearing a painful exposure. But anyone working and living in truth and reality welcomes God-light so the work can be seen for the God-work it is."*

Our journey requires we move toward light and truth in order to examine our behaviors and expand our understanding because God holds us accountable. Bringing our issues into the light and exposing them may feel humiliating. Let me assure you it is a necessary step in the surgical process of restoration. It brings about healing.

Our objective is to get in touch with our *real* selves, the part of us we've hidden away for so long. Unless we make a strenuous effort to face, and be rid of, all the destructive and negative things within ourselves, our decision to submit and turn our lives over to the care of God will have little meaning.

The Twelve Step program calls this a "moral inventory" because it concerns our behavior. I call it our "immoral inventory" because it includes the seven deadly sins and behaviors such as lying, fear, toxic thoughts, dishonesty, impatience, and gossiping. We must examine our inventory and look at patterns if we want to get out of this stuck place. Looking at and taking responsibility for our behaviors will give us the freedom to live our lives as God intended.

This exercise requires us to settle the past. This means *complete honesty* about who we really are and what we've done. Socrates said the unexamined life is not worth living. We need deep, spiritual changes. I say we must risk undoing who we've become in order to live the life we desire.

In the Old Testament, the high priests were instructed to *"spend the day in self-examination and humility . . .for this is the day commemorating the atonement, cleansing you in the Lord's eyes from all of your sins" (Leviticus 16:29-30, TLB)*. The New Testament says, *"Examine yourselves to see whether you are in the faith; test yourselves (2 Corinthians 13:5)*. We will only benefit in proportion to the amount of honesty we bring into the self-examination process.

Death to Self

Elbert Hubbard said, "We are not punished for our sins, but by them."[27] No question, letting go of what is pleasurable and familiar is difficult. Those nasty habits resurface. The toxic thoughts recur. Sin keeps climbing back onto its throne. The attitude, "I'll stop the behavior and replace it with something else (and ignore the root cause)," isn't usually effective.

To stop the cycle, we must work to free ourselves from the root desires. We must look at the internal cause rather than focus only on the action. It's great if we can replace a toxic obsession with a healthy passion. But if we don't find out why, then most likely we'll end up playing musical addictions.

The image the New Testament uses for getting rid of our sinful behavior is the one of crucifixion—a slow, painful suffocating of self. Galatians 5:24 says, *"Those who belong to Christ Jesus crucify the sinful nature with its passions and desires."*

I think too often this is one of those biblical truths which have been misapplied. Taken out of context it results in a narrow and faulty doctrine that says, "If you really want to follow Christ you must give up your comfortable life to suffer and be miserable. The more you suffer, the more God will love you."

Jesus meant we must accept the death of our own self-directed life. This can be very difficult because it's hard to be honest with ourselves. It's hard to give up our attachments. And we can only do it through the outworking of our faith. I, for one, have not reached the point of complete death to self.

God will help us get honest with ourselves. If we don't, we cannot grow spiritually. When we crucify our sinful nature, we commit to work constantly at identifying our character deficiencies: faults, blemishes, shortcomings, sins. We begin our pursuit for righteousness—the things that are pleasing to God—and we ask God to help us get rid of them. The result is a life of love, joy, peace, self-discipline, and other fruits of the spirit. I can tell you first-hand, this is a great life!

Denial has been the operative word in our life. Now God will open our eyes to the weaknesses that need changing. When we ask the Holy Spirit to go to work in us, He redirects all the destructive into the constructive—

into healthy, positive, and life-affirming activities. He will build on our strengths.

~

The wise King Soloman stated, *"There is a time for everything"* (Ecclesiastes 3:1). The air of our life is musty. Shameful secrets, embarrassing behaviors, lost hope, all hidden from view. We've been afraid to open the doors to anyone because we may be found out, rejected, and further shamed. It's time to clean house!

This scares some of us. For others, you cannot wait to be free of the mess.

This is a purification process and an exercise in humility to find out what we must throw out (to change) to have a more serene and productive life. To achieve this goal, we must examine our lives to date: the negative characteristics that have caused us so much pain, as well as our assets.

Begin to walk down each aisle of your life. What do you see? Consider all aspects—relational, physical, emotional, and spiritual. Note areas of strength and weakness. With regard to relationships, take note of hurts and resentments. Examine healthy and loving relationships. Note the negative and the positive ways you communicate with others.

Since multiple addictions are the rule rather than the exception, name what you believe yours are. If you haven't already, make a commitment to deal with them as you go forward. When these other hidden addictions are not purged, recovery may be hindered. The toxicity will rear its ugly head in no time. Look to God for guidance so you can leave each wound at the cross and strengthen each asset.

Day Five: Choose a Confidante

It is the confession, not the priest, that gives us absolution. –Oscar Wilde

'Coming clean' breaks the power behind a stronghold.

We're now required to engage in an honest confrontation by admitting our faults to God, to ourselves, and to at least one other person. OUCH! *We must do this.*

Prayerful sharing with a sister or brother in Christ prepares the way for restoration. James 5:16 says,

"Confess your sins to each other and pray for each other so that you may be healed. The earnest prayer of a righteous person has great power and produces wonderful results" (NLT).

Recall Proverbs 28:13 says, *"He who conceals his sins does not prosper, but whoever confesses and renounces them finds mercy."*

Confession is incredibly liberating. Not only do you transfer the weight of these faults from you to God, but He promises to forgive and cleanse you as he removes your transgressions. By confessing our wrongs, we begin the important phase of setting aside our pride so we can see ourselves truthfully.

Bearing the burden of our wrongdoings drains us of vital energy. Confession will renew our energy level. We're humbled when we admit we're wrong. Yet we also experience courage which begets strength and freedom. With strength comes recovery!

This is an ego-deflating experience. I know! Admission to another person can make our secrets and faults real and more painful. Yet, the humility that comes from confiding our toxic thoughts and behaviors to someone else is one of the greatest rewards in healing.

This spells f-r-e-e-d-o-m.

You are free to work with anyone you please. Pray. Find someone you can trust, who is understanding and compassionate. This person should not only listen but encourage and edify. Thank God for this friend who knows and accepts that you're not perfect, who helps you see your mistakes, and won't give up on you.

Rigorous Honesty

Humility says, "God I need your grace! I'll do my best but the outcome is up to you alone." Are you too ashamed to confess your behavior? Are you fearful of humiliation? That wouldn't be unusual which is why we need a lot of prayer.

God makes you a promise, *"Do not be afraid; you will not suffer shame. Do not fear disgrace; you will not be humiliated" (Isaiah 54:4–8).* Satan will tell you that you have much to be ashamed of. He'll tell you that you'll humiliate yourself.

Remember, you have the authority to tell Satan he is a liar. Say, "Satan, it is written: *'When I am afraid, I will trust in God. In God, whose Word I praise, in God I trust; I will not be afraid. What can mortal man [and you Satan] do to me?' (Psalm 56:3–4)* Nothing! God tells me that His unfailing love for me will not be shaken because He has compassion on me (Isaiah 54:10)."

The goal of this exercise is to search for patterns of thinking and behavior that have served us badly. It's an examination of our lives, of sin, in the loving presence of God. This exercise initiates the restoration of our personal integrity by forcing us to remove our masks. 1 John 1:8–10 says,

> *"If we claim to be without sin, we deceive ourselves and the truth is not in us. If we confess our sins, he is faithful and just and will forgive us our sins and purify us from all unrighteousness. If we claim we have not sinned, we make him out to be a liar and his word has no place in our lives."*

Self-deception is human nature. Romans 3:23 says, *"For all have sinned and fall short of the glory of God."* We're being challenged to be honest. The work we're doing makes us realize just how far we've fallen short of God's plan. But there is great news. God wipes our dirty, tarnished slate clean. Praise God!

Closing Moments

How do you feel right now?

The work we've done has started the process of relieving the guilt and shame that has enveloped our lives for so long. The consequences of our actions are our responsibility. Humbly ask God for guidance. *Thy will, not mine, be done.*

The temptation is to pray a general prayer and ask God to remove everything as if it were a nice, neat little package. Pray for the removal of each deficiency and sin (that you are aware of) one at a time. The manner and timing of the amputations (this is what it feels like) is up to God, not us.

We will soon find once we accept God's care and control, our fears lessen. We begin to experience love and joy in our lives.

"Repent, then, and turn to God, so that your sins may be wiped out, that times of refreshing may come from the Lord" (Acts 3:19). We're being called to repent, to turn around and reorient our heart and lives. Our desire is to live in a radically new way—in the light of the kingdom Jesus introduced into the world.

Promise to Claim: And we know that in all things God works for the good of those who love him, who have been called according to his purpose. (Romans 8:28)

Week 7

Heal for Life

When was the last time you felt *really* alive?

Joy is one of God's greatest medicines. Once we make restitution and receive God's forgiveness, our healing and restoration takes place. Joy can finally replace guilt, shame, rejection, fear, and all of those ugly emotions.

> *"You turned my wailing into dancing; you removed my sack-cloth and clothed me with joy, that my heart may sing to you and not be silent. O Lord my God, I will give you thanks forever" (Psalm 16:11).*

This is David's response after he accepted God's forgiveness. God wants the same for us. He not only wants to fill us with peace and joy, but He wants us to be so full of Him that we over- flow with His joy and hope for our future 1 Peter 1:6-8 describes being filled with an "inexpressible joy":

> *"So be truly glad! There is wonderful joy ahead, even though the going is rough for a while down here. These trials are only to test your faith, to see whether or not it's strong and pure. It's being tested as fire tests gold and purifies it—and your faith is far more precious to God than mere gold; so if your faith remains strong after being tried in the test tube of fiery trials, it will bring you much praise and glory and honor on the day of his return. You love him even though you have never seen him; though not seeing him, you trust him; and even now you are happy with the inexpressible joy that comes from heaven itself" (TLB).*

Peter is describing a very real feeling of joy and encouragement. This comes from knowing we don't have to endure our pain and struggles alone. God is with us, even when we cannot see Him. He continues to give us courage and strength to persevere. God helps us see that our trials serve His purpose. They move us down His path toward greater faith and a healthier life.

Joy brings into focus our distorted perceptions. Even in the war zones of life, there is joy because our God is great, and we're bathed in His love. The joy Jesus gives us isn't grounded in our circumstances—it's grounded in Him. When we fix our eyes on Jesus we find in Him authentic joy.

- Joy is healthy.
- Joy is freeing.
- Joy is contagious.
- Joy makes us alive!

Day One: Break Free from Social Pressures

Happiness is a by-product of a healthy attitude. And a healthy attitude is one that takes the normal turmoil of life and mixes it with a belief in God's presence.

–Unknown

Are you doing what you were born to do?

The book title *You're Born an Original, Don't Die a Copy* by John Mason says it all. God Almighty only creates originals—not duplicates. *"I make all things new,"* He declares (Revelation 21:5). You haven't been mass-produced. You're a one of a kind—you-nique! Yet we lose our way because we're given so many conflicting messages to process.

Over time most of us have felt forced to conform to what our culture and family told us to be. Granted Christians cannot completely disentangle themselves from the real world. We still remain enmeshed in it. Yet 1 Peter 1:14 says, *"Don't slip back into your old ways of living to satisfy your own desires"* (NLT).

Part of the restoration process is breaking free from these social pressures—the pressures to be thin, to look a certain way, to attain a certain status, and to be perfect. We're being asked to think and live as nonconformists, refusing to yield to the pressures that lead us to ungodly living. Paul explains how to be free of sociocultural influences:

"Therefore, I urge you, brothers, in view of God's mercy, to offer your bodies as living sacrifices, holy and pleasing to God—this is your spiritual act of worship. Do not conform any longer to the pattern of this world, but be transformed by the renewing of your mind. Then you will be able to test and approve what God's will is—his good, pleasing and perfect will" (Romans 12:1–2).

What do you think Paul means when he says we are to "offer our bodies to God?" Eugene Peterson's *The Message* translates this passage,

"So here's what I want you to do, God helping you: Take your everyday, ordinary life—your sleeping, eating, going-to-work, and walking-around life—and place it before God as an offering. Embracing what God does for you is the best thing you can do for him. Don't become so well-adjusted to your culture that you fit into it without even thinking. Instead, fix your attention on God. You'll be changed from the inside out. Readily recognize what he wants from you, and quickly respond to it. Unlike the culture around you, always dragging you down to its level of immaturity, God brings the best out of you, develops well-formed maturity in you."

You are one of a kind—designed to glorify God as only you can.

God doesn't want us to copy the behavior and habits of this world because it only turns us into slaves. He wants us to be a new and different person—in everything we do and think. We'll experience how His ways can ultimately satisfy us, not our self-centered ways.

Real Freedom

Could it be possible that you've become so used to living in bondage that you may be resisting freedom?

The Israelites were slaves for four hundred years. Moses was the one who came to tell them they could be free. But the Israelites were more concerned about what their masters would do that they missed what God's freedom would bring. Freedom for them meant that Pharaoh would be angry, therefore, the Egyptians would attack them. Freedom didn't seem worth the price.

Sometimes we feel this way. But our feelings must be over-ridden with truth. Galatians 5:1 states,

"It's for freedom that Christ has [past tense] *set us free. Stand firm, then,* [a present tense command] *and do not let yourselves be burdened again* [like in your past life] *by a yoke of slavery."*

Christ has already liberated us from the bondage in which we were born—not to bring us into another form of bondage, but to free us completely. We are all products of our past, but we don't have to be prisoners of our past.

Day Two: Victory Over Temptations and Triggers

As a dog returns to its vomit, so a fool repeats his foolishness. –Proverbs 26:11 (NLT)

We cannot escape temptation and booby traps.

A *temptation* is an enticement by Satan that always includes sin and is aimed at bringing us down. A *trigger* is a signal, a temptation, which, for example, precedes a binge or compulsive overeating episode. Giving in to either is saying something else is more desirable than God and His ways.

For example, every day we're blasted with hundreds of media messages which produce thousands of tempting and fearful thoughts. Often, temptation equals relapse if we don't stand strong with God. But the difference is that in Christ, we have the strength to resist temptation that we never had before. Because Jesus experienced temptation when He suffered, He's able to help us when we're tempted.

Even with Christ in our lives, we are not immune from temptation. There will always be certain situations that make us vulnerable: advertisements for diets, cosmetic procedures, and fitness products and services. Learning to recognize manipulative messages and navigate through temptations and triggers is part of the work.

It's imperative that we carefully examine the living and working environment that enables addictive behaviors. Think: what are the persons, places, things, and stresses that nurture the toxic thinking and behaviors?

The Scriptures use Israel's history as a warning about the perils of temptation. Paul relates that despite God's abundant blessing, the nation nevertheless chose the wrong pathway. The Israelites were tempted and they yielded, filling their lives with idols. In fact, that nation's entire history was a recurring cycle of obedience, blessing, temptation, and rebellion (see 1 Corinthians 10:1–12). God promises us help when we encounter temptation:

- 1 Corinthians 10:13: *"No temptation has seized you except what is common to man. And God is faithful; he will not let you be tempted beyond what you can bear. But when you are tempted, he will also provide a way out so that you can stand up under it."*
- Titus 2:11–12: *"For the grace of God that brings salvation has appeared to all men. It teaches us to say "No" to ungodliness and worldly passions, and to live self-controlled, upright, and godly lives in this present age."*

He tells us what to do to overcome temptation:

- Matthew 26:41: *"Watch and pray so that you will not fall into temptation."*
- Ephesians 6:13: *"Therefore put on the full armor of God, so that when the day of evil comes, you may be able to stand your ground, and after you have done everything, to stand."*

Martin Luther once said, "You cannot keep the birds from flying over your head, but you can keep them from building a nest in your hair." Temptation will pester you, but temptation doesn't have to master you.

Ask yourself, "If I should yield to this temptation, what will be the immediate and future consequence to me and those around me? Am I prepared to pay the price? Is there a better way to get this need met?"

Some circumstances will cause you to fall immediately. These situations are unique to your weaknesses. You must identify them because Satan already knows them and has a plan to lead you into those traps. Pray for discernment start to identify and record patterns of temptation. Be prepared to confront those situations.

Day Three: Walk in God-Confidence

Self-confidence looks inward—God-confidence looks upward. –Donna Partow

God is gently helping us to discard our masks.

Now we can come out from behind the curtain for the big "reveal" and present our real self to others . . . and ourselves. People will always reject us, discourage us, not accept us, and give us a reason to want to put the masks back on. However, God will continue to show us in His loving way that our masks are simply not necessary anymore.

God loved you enough to make you exactly the way He wanted you to be—*in His image* (Genesis 1:27). Positive self-image comes from this knowledge; and God healing and changing our hearts and minds. He gives us God-confidence, which is different from self-confidence. When we have self-confidence, we believe we have the power to do almost anything. We go it alone. When we gain God-confidence, we believe we have the power to do anything—through Him. There's a big difference.

Someone said, "The best makeup is a smile. The best jewelry is modesty. The best clothing is confidence." I believe people noticed me when I acquired God-confidence. Nothing on the outside of me was different. I appeared to display a radiant glow from the inside that came from spending time with Jesus. Peter spoke about biblical women who were beautiful because they reflected their inner self, which meant they lived a God-directed and respectful existence.

When a woman follows God's direction, she receives a special inner beauty that is reflected in her outward appearance. People may not know why she's beautiful. In fact, some may say, "She's not what we call a beauty (by our cultural standards), but there is something about her; some sort of spiritual glow."

Man cannot fix a lot of our problems. When we turn to God and seek His advice and counsel He gives us God-confidence. We have what it takes to make those critical life changes. If we choose to put our confidence in God, we know the solution will be the right solution.

Accept Yourself

You've made great progress toward wholeness! Now you can start to *really* live again. Today, do you feel you can fully accept yourself the way you are? If you said no then pray and ask God to show you how you can begin to accept yourself. Dr. Gregory Jantz wrote,

"When you can accept yourself, you can laugh again—at yourself and others. Your happiness will no longer be based upon the opinions and desires of other people. Fear of rejection by others will no longer hold you prisoner, because you no longer reject yourself and your past. You are learning to really *like* who you are. Perfectionism has shadowed your life. Now reality can help you see yourself clearly. You have learned that it's okay and *perfectly* normal to make mistakes."[28]

We've all heard the saying, "Garbage in. Garbage out." We want to put a plug in our "garbage in" vestibule. This means we say no to, for example, celebrity-oriented and extreme makeover programming. If you know that when you open a magazine full of expensively dressed, skinny, beautiful women that it will make you feel bad about yourself, then walk away from or throw the magazine away.

We want to focus daily on Jesus and not the comparison game that the world plays. You can either live in fear of the dreaded "pooch" and wrinkles, or live your life for God. *Perfection never lasts—but character lasts forever.*

Day Four: Restoring God's Temple

It's the glow within that creates beauty. People are like stained glass windows. They sparkle like crystal in the sun. At night they continue to sparkle only if there is light within. —Unknown

Your body is God's temple.

"Do you not know that your body is a temple of the Holy Spirit, who is in you, whom you have received from God? You are not your own; you were bought at a price. Therefore honor God with your body" (1 Corinthians 6:19–20).

Before we were Christians, we were all slaves to sin. When we decided to follow Jesus, we stepped out in faith, made Jesus our Lord, and became His. Then His Spirit came to dwell in us. This means our bodies are for the Lord. They are to be an instrument of righteousness and holiness, not an instrument of abuse. Paul shows us the effect of being a slave to sin had on our lives in the past:

"Just as you used to offer the parts of your body in slavery to impurity and to ever-increasing wickedness, so now offer them in slavery to righteousness leading to holiness. When you were slaves to sin, you were free from the control of righteousness. What benefit did you reap at that time from the things you are now ashamed of? Those things result in death! But now that you have been set free from sin and have become slaves to God, the benefit you reap leads to holiness, and the result is eternal life. For the wages of sin is death, but the gift of God is eternal life in Christ Jesus our Lord" (Romans 6:19–23).

Did you hear that? You've been set free from sin and have become a slave to something good—to righteousness.

Experience Victory

Victory is possible when we start to change the way we think and realize we are both beautiful on the inside as well as the outside. *How can we experience real victory ...*

- *Over the flesh?* 2 Corinthians 10:5: *"We demolish arguments and every pretension that sets itself up against the knowledge of God, and we take captive every thought to make it obedient to Christ."*

- *Over Satan?* By putting on the full armor of God. Use your authority as a believer in Jesus Christ to directly deal with him. Confront Satan out loud because he cannot read your mind as God can (remember, he's a created being). Say something like, "Satan, in the name and authority of Jesus, I command you to get away from me. My victory and honor come from God alone. He's my refuge, a rock where no enemy can reach me (Psalm 62:7)."

- *Over the world?* 1 John 2:15–17 says, *"Do not love the world or anything in the world."* Jesus knows we cannot spend day after day in this society without it affecting our minds, hearts, and souls. They become unguarded and start to imperceptibly shift away from God. This is why He's given us his Word—to permeate our thinking so we do not become conformed to our culture's practices.

God tells us to *live by the Spirit* so we won't gratify the desires of the sinful nature (Galatians 5:16). The power to live a sanctified life comes only when we plug into God's unlimited power. Daily, we seek His face and ask to be filled more with the Holy Spirit. The Spirit will give us the desire to hear, digest, and obey God's Word.

Day Five: Evaluating Friendships

Friends are the support players who usually require fewer emotional supplies than family members and who help us with our problems. —Brenda Hunter

Most of us have been so obsessed with food, our bodies, and other worldly things that we've had little time for mending and building relationships. Healing means we cannot go it alone. God designed us to connect with others. Connecting is life.

Now is the time to survey our relationships. We have a God-given need to have our love tanks filled by family, community, and peer support. If we choose to isolate, then we cannot be filled sufficiently.

In today's busy, overfilled world many women have few or no friends. We must evaluate and most likely enlarge our circle of friends. This scared me. I believed I'd be rejected (again) because I'd always mess up relationships. We must realize we are now working from a new viewpoint with different motivations.

No question intimacy is risky. We think, *If I reach out to another woman there's a chance she may reject me. If I trust my deepest, darkest secrets to another woman, she may pull back in shock, or even worst, tell others.* It may sound like too much work to let people in and cultivate friendships. We don't have to have a lot of friends. We need at least one person we can count on. If a woman has just one trustworthy friend, she's protected from depression when she experiences significant life stress.[29]

Jesus said, *"Love each other in the same way I have loved you. There is no greater love than to lay down one's life for one's friends" (John 15:12-13, NLT).* Jesus desires we be connected to others. Once we embrace friendship then we become that much needed genuine friend to other women, helping them out of the dark valley into the light. God designed life for intimacy, not isolation. Ecclesiastes 4:8-12 says,

"Also, on a cold night, two under the same blanket gain warmth from each other, but how can one be warm alone? And one standing alone can be attacked and defeated, but two can stand back-to-back and conquer; three is even better, for a triple-braided cord is not easily broken" (TLB).

As we learn to reach out to God and others, they will meet us, and new friendships will take root and grow. I call these *divine appointments*.

If you are single: God designed us to be loved intimately and tenderly by another person for a lifetime. Yet this kind of love can be one of the most painful to endure. So, for right now we're going to make new decisions about male relationships. We must heal before jumping into a new romantic relationship. Let me say at this point: if you are a codependent I urge you to seek healing in this area of your life. There are many good Christ-based books on the subject.

The term *codependency* refers to a relationship where one or both parties enable the other person to act in certain maladaptive ways. The codependent person is emotionally about 50 percent available. She has built-in radar that leads her to other half available persons in an attempt to make a whole person. The word codependent literally means "dependent with." The opposite of codependency is "interdependent."

Closing Moments

There is joy in the morning.

Whether we realize it or not, we have many things to be joyful for:

- If you woke up this morning with more health than illness, you're more blessed than the million people who won't survive the week.

- If you have never experienced the danger of battle, the loneliness of imprisonment, the agony of torture, or the pangs of starvation, you're better off than 20 million people around the world.

- If you attend church without fear of harassment, arrest, torture, or death, you're more blessed than almost three billion people in the world.

- If you have food in your refrigerator, clothes on your back, a roof over your head, and a place to sleep, you're richer than 75 percent of this world.

- If you have money in the bank and in your wallet, you're among the top eight percent of the world's wealthy.

- If your parents are still married, you're very rare, especially in America.

- If you hold up your head with a smile on your face and are truly thankful, you're blessed because the majority can, but most do not.

- If you can hold someone's hand, hug them, or touch them on the shoulder, you're blessed because you can offer God's healing touch.

- If you can read this, you're more blessed than over two billion people in the world that cannot read anything at all.

Promise to Claim: So, if the Son sets you free, you will be free indeed.
(John 8:36)

Week 8

Nourish and Nurture God's Temple

How do you feel about food right?

Now that you've made such great progress toward wholeness, is food your friend or foe? Emotional eating involves two sets of issues and behaviors: those involving relationships with others and ourselves, and those relating to food and nutrition.

The first 7-weeks focused on the first issue. If you haven't read and applied the work of the previous weeks, it would not be wise to continue. The principles probably won't work until you can say that you now love yourself and the transformation process has begun.

Many of us could write books about nutrition and diets. Obsessed with food, I majored in nutrition in college. Restoration isn't about developing a new weight-loss program or coming up with a new way to control our eating. *Been there, done that.* With God's help, we can assume greater control as we begin the journey toward new and better habits. We must first decide that food is a source of nutrition, not a drug; a source of sustenance, not pleasure.

After 16 years of bingeing and purging and starving, I didn't know what it was like to eat like a normal person—to eat when I was hungry and for the nutritional value. I ate in secrecy. Don't all of have a secret hiding place? We eat and binge there. We hide and hoard food there when everyone's gone to bed. We hide like a criminal there. Proverbs 9:17–18 says,

"Stolen water is sweet; food eaten in secret is delicious! But little do they know that the dead are there, that her guests are in the depths of the grave."

God knows what we do in secrecy and hates that it's destroying us. He has the answers. He can help us to relearn the art of eating regular meals again—meals that provide much needed strength and stamina.

Jesus said (the Lord's Prayer, Matthew 6:11), "Give us today our daily bread." In other words, "Lord, please give me today that which I need for this very day."

Speak it out: "With God's help I will give my body the best care and most nutritious food I can."

Day One: Care for Your Body

The mind is the driver of change but your body is the vehicle that gets you there.
—Dr. Gregory L. Jantz

Our health needs to be an ongoing priority.

God put every one of us on this earth to fulfill an assignment. How can we fill our assignments if we're weak, undernourished, overweight, and not healthy? We must be healthy in order to be strong.

The Old Testament (Genesis 5) tells us that many of God's people lived to a ripe, old age—some nine hundred years old! The older women were fertile and men were virile (Genesis 21:1–8). Do you ever wonder why? Dr. Patrick Quillan wrote,

"Scientists have been accumulating data, which proves the merits of the biblical diet and lifestyle. We were created by God with certain physical requirements. If we do not meet these needs, then the body does not function well. After years of struggling to perform in spite of poor conditions, the body eventually gives out in disease and early death. *But don't blame God. God gave us free will to make our own choices in life.*"[30]

First Corinthians 8:9 warns us, *"Be careful, however, that the exercise of your freedom does not become a stumbling block to the weak."* Sadly, we have misused our freedom and chosen the wrong foods and lifestyle. Trusted nutrition expert, Gregory Jantz said that "when your physical body is supported, it can help you find the self-confidence and encouragement to deal with the important emotional, relational, and spiritual issues that need to be addressed in your long-term recovery."[31]

There is an age-old saying that God feeds the birds, but He doesn't throw the food into their nests. The birds must get their own food. The point is we're expected to do our part—to partner with God to bring about health and longevity. *"For we are God's fellow workers; you are God's field, God's building"* (1 Corinthians 3:9).

Day Two: God's Covenant

The biggest seller is cookbooks and the second is diet books—how not to eat what you've just learned to cook. –Andy Rooney

Is food a blessing or for filling the void?

Did you know that in Abraham's era, food was a visible means of knowing that there was a God? Both animals and plants provided food. Thanksgiving was offered at each meal because they connected food with God. Food was a sign of God's generosity and a symbol of His miraculous power.

Jesus is represented in the symbol of a fish. He converted water into wine for His first miracle (John 2:9). Jesus used bread and wine in the Passover Feast as symbols of His body and blood to be sacrificed (Luke 22:19–21). Food was a covenant between God and His people. When the Israelites were wandering in the desert, God sent them "manna" (Exodus 16:31–32). Manna was new to their diet and gave them much nourishment.

God also used the manna as an instrument to teach the Israelites an important lesson, a lesson for us too. *"Each morning everyone gathered as much as he needed, and when the sun grew hot, it melted away"* (Exodus 16:21). The key is "daily." The Israelites asked for what they needed on a daily basis. God wants to be with us on a daily basis. Don't wait for the outward need. He wants us to ask Him for our desires and needs every day.

Today, most of us look at food as something to fill the void in our soul—something to control and provide immediate gratification and pleasure. However, that feeling doesn't make our problems go away. Some think God will love them more if they eat the food He's blessed them with. So, they overeat. These are traps! If we eat this way—to fill the void or to please God, we've ignored God's purpose for providing food—to nourish our body with essential nutrients and connect to Him. Meditate on this verse:

"He humbled you, causing you to hunger and then feeding you with manna, which neither you nor your fathers had known, to teach you that man does not live on bread alone but on every word that comes from the mouth of the Lord" (Deuteronomy 8:3).

Day Three: Fight for the New You

We live by inner statements that are born out of experienced pain, and these statements shape our lives more than we can possibly imagine. —Paula Rinehart

Have you thought about an action plan?

Most likely, you know how you should eat, but you probably find it too difficult to put that knowledge into practice. Dr. Jantz advises,

"I never ask anyone to go on a diet. Both the initial and ultimate false premise of a diet is that *food is the culprit.* Food is not the problem, and, therefore, food is not the cure. The antidote to dieting—is to live a truly authentic, balanced, healthy life as a person who is growing into the individual God created you to be."[32]

An actress popular in the 50's said, "I've been on a diet for two weeks, and all I've lost is fourteen days." Statistically, diets usually equal failure, and they emphasize what's wrong instead of what's right. They encourage competition and comparison.

If you are like me, you will most likely hate your new food plan—initially. We hate change and discipline, don't we? Again, we are asked to submit ourselves to doing something God's way. Paul said,

"Like an athlete I punish my body, treating it roughly, training it to do what it should, not what it wants to." We're making our bodies our slave, instead of us being a slave to our bodies" (1 Corinthians 9:27, TLB).

Speak It Out

I hope "Speak It Out" is part of your daily routine. You can apply it as you make the change to a healthy food plan. When you feel tempted and weak, pull out your favorite verses and inspirational quotes. Tape them to your refrigerator or your computer at work, any place where you are most vulnerable. We need God to help us every day. If you don't have any favorite verses, select a few of these and personalize them:

- *"He gives strength to the weary and increases the power of the weak"* (Isaiah 40:29). God gives me strength and power when I'm weak.

- *"Commit to the Lord whatever you do, and your plans will succeed"* (Proverbs 16:3). I commit my food plan to you, Father. I will succeed!

- *"The Lord will fight for you; you need only to be still"* (Exodus 14:14). The Lord is fighting for me, I just need to relax and rest in Him.

- *"This is my work, and I can do it only because Christ's mighty energy is at work within me"* (Colossians 1:29, TLB).

- *"The Lord is a strong fortress. The godly run to him and are safe"* (Proverbs 18:10, TLB). The Lord is my fortification. He will get me through my plan today.

Change is tough. Try to view it as medicine. At first, it's unpleasant to take, but it eventually restores strength and wholeness.

Visualize a Healthier You

Imagine where you want to be. "Visualization," also referred to as "guided imagery," is a mental rehearsal technique often used in sports. Brain studies reveal that thoughts produce the same mental instructions as actions. For some, it's an extremely powerful tool. Many people use it to change image, diet, and exercise habits. They visualize a positive outcome or scenario. (As Christians, we call it *belief* and *faith*.)

Stress is a major trigger. Emotional stress is always the demon that drives us to seek solace in false fixes like food. According to *MayoClinic.com*, practicing visualization as a form of meditation can help to relieve stress and put you back into a calm frame of mind.[33]

Why not give it a try? Spend 5 to 10 minutes a day visualizing yourself making healthier eating choices. You can do this in the morning after your prayer and devotion time. Or in the shower as you get ready for work .... whatever works for you.

Ask God to help you calm your mind and help you visualize fully. *"I can do everything through him who gives me strength"* (Philippians 4:13). I have God's strength. I can follow this plan!

Day Four: Healthy Eating and Exercise

No discipline seems pleasant at the time, but painful. Later on, however, it produces a harvest of righteousness and peace for those who have been trained by it.
—Paul, speaking in Hebrews 12:11

Why do certain foods seem to be addictive?

Do you receive comfort from eating certain foods like pasta, pizza, macaroni, ice cream, chocolate, or bread? Do certain meals trigger increased eating frequency? If you answered yes, there is a reason. Scientific evidence indicates certain foods are addictive and should be avoided (see *The Dopamine Makes Me Do It* on page 11). Food manufacturers have studied this. They know that after repeated exposure to these kinds of food, a person can become addicted to them. The best advice: avoid these addictive foods altogether (I know, easier said than done).

Professionals say that when we live and participate in an active social community, are surrounded by healthy foods and opportunities for exercise, the genes that control weight will operate as God intended. We can enjoy a fit and healthy body.

Moderation

God wants balance in your life, and one area is eating in moderation. (If you're still overpowered by food addiction, moderation most likely will be hard. Don't give up! Keep applying what you've been learning.) The concept is scriptural.

- Proverbs 23:1–3: *"When you sit to dine with a ruler, note well what is before you, and put a knife to your throat if you are given to gluttony. Do not crave his delicacies, for that food is deceptive."*

- Proverbs 25:16: *"If you find honey, eat just enough—too much of it, and you will vomit."*

In Daniel 1, King Nebuchadnezzar took the Israelites hostage. The king provided well for the hostages. He offered them a royal feast. Verse 5 says, "The king assigned them a daily amount of food and wine from the king's table." When the king offered such delicacies to Daniel, *"Daniel resolved not to defile himself with the royal food and wine, and he asked the chief official for permission not to defile himself this way"* (1:8).

What does "not to defile himself" mean? Daniel made a personal decision about what he would eat. Unlike many of us, he didn't let food define who he was. He decided what was good for him, his total body, and soul. Since the king's delicacies had been offered to idols, Daniel knew those delicacies were not good for him (body and soul). He successfully resisted the lure of the world and experienced the rewards of God's favor.

Daniel triumphed because he made up his mind not to eat the food (1:8). He succeeded because he made a vow ahead of time to avoid worldly temptations.

Metabolism

Your metabolism (the amount of energy you burn) goes up and down depending on how much you eat. If you're trying to lose weight, and you only eat one meal a day with a snack, you may be lowering your metabolism. This makes it harder for your body to lose weight.

Think of your metabolism like a fire. In order to get the fire going, you must start with small pieces (kindling) so the fire can build. As it gets hotter and stronger, you add big pieces (logs). But you wouldn't start the fire with a log, would you? The best way to raise your metabolism so you can eat more food without gaining weight is by eating smaller, more frequent meals. This is how I eat now.

Exercise

Some of you are compulsive over-exercisers, and others think a dumbbell is an idiot. I used to be the first. It wasn't unusual for me to get up at 3 or 4 a.m. to exercise. I'd feel extremely guilty for missing a workout. As a jogger, my knees took an intense pounding day after day. Consequently, I had two arthroscopic surgeries on both knees. I experienced other injuries, anxiety, amenorrhea, bone loss, and a drop-in protein levels due to the intensity of exercise. I refused to allow my body time to rest and recover.

God didn't design our bodies to run daily marathons, even though everyone at the gym praises the accomplishment. As my thinking began to change, my rigid regimen began to relax. I could see how compulsive my routine was. It's important to exercise, but it's also important to listen to your body and not take it to extremes. Believe me—you will pay for it later.

For those of you who hate exercise, it may be because you see exercise as a set of rules that cannot be broken (like a diet). Yes, God has rules for holy living, but throw out any preconceived rules about exercise. Regular physical activity is important. It builds muscle or lean body mass, improves body toning, strength, and bone density. Aerobic exercise strengthens the heart and lung muscles. Exercise can also lead to higher brain functioning.

Exercise directly regenerates D2-like dopamine receptors—similar to those linked with food addiction—in the brain, helping to rebuild the damage of past addiction and prevent it in the future. You don't have to join a gym. Begin by simply walking. A five-minute walk around the block or 30 jumping jacks reduces the intensity of withdrawal symptoms.[34]

If you are extremely thin, or have been diagnosed with anorexia, or have abused exercise, your doctor or therapist may advise you *not* to exercise for a while for health reasons.

Day Five: A Healthy Diet

We first make our habits, and then our habits make us. –John Dryden

Talk with a professional before starting any new eating plan. Enlist the help of a family member or friend to give you support and help you stay on track. The challenge is to create an eating plan that you can live with and includes healthy foods. *"When dining with a rich man, be on your guard and don't stuff yourself, though it all tastes so good"* (Proverbs 23:1, TLB).

Steps to good nutrition come from a diet that:[35]

- Is balanced with foods from all groups that include several servings of fruits and vegetables (a variety of each, five to nine servings each day), and grains (especially whole grains, a good source of fiber).

- Is low in saturated fat and cholesterol, and moderate in total fat intake. Less than 10 percent of your daily calories should come from saturated fat, and less than 30 percent of your daily calories should come from total fat.

- Has a limited number of calories from sugars (candy, cookies, and cakes).

- Has foods prepared with less sodium or salt—no more than 2,400 milligrams of sodium per day, or about one teaspoon of salt per day for a healthy heart.

- Does not rely on a lot of processed and pre-packaged foods.

Fasting and Bingeing

As Christians, fasting can be an excellent spiritual discipline. Yet, I would caution you against fasting until you've completely healed from emotional eating. *What if I binge?*

When I started following a healthy food plan, some days I desired a second serving or a desert. In my mind, I knew it was okay once in a while, but Satan would bait me. He knew I promised myself I wouldn't purge, so he cunningly told me I should take laxatives instead to get rid of the fat. I came to learn that laxatives didn't do this. I'd tell him, "Satan, this is *not* an option! Go away!"

I discovered my body could digest more food than I thought. I used to think that if I went one ounce over my food plan, I'd gain a couple pounds. Guess what? I didn't! If I go out to lunch and eat more than I'm comfortable with, I listen to my stomach. Usually, I only want a small dinner. My body compensates for the change and I don't gain extra weight.

Have a Relapse Plan

What do you think your chances of relapse are? I believe it depends on the seriousness of your addiction, whether you caught it in the early stages or much later. Addictions tend to be chronic and progressive, therefore relapsing. Many of us still tend to respond to the old shame-based and self-hatred messages. You may need to recycle through this healing study again. Asking myself these questions about my motives for eating has worked for me. They point to the reasons I binge.

- Am I really hungry, or is it because I'm bored, stressed, angry, fearful, or depressed?
- Is an event fueling my desire to binge?
- Have I had enough sleep and exercise?
- How did I rationalize my behavior?
- What were some of the messages I said to myself—were they shame-based, anxiety or fear-driven?

I have a support network of a few friends to call when I'm feeling vulnerable. I also realize I must continually affirm my self-worth. Writing Scripture-based positive affirmations about myself is valuable. I pray and repeat Scripture: *"How sweet are your words to my taste, sweeter than honey [bingeing] to my mouth!" (Psalm 119:103)*

If you relapse, forgive yourself. Throw the monkey of guilt and shame off your back. This is normal. *It's progress, not perfection. It's okay to fall down and be imperfect.*

Laxative Withdrawal

Laxative withdrawal is especially difficult for people struggling with an eating disorder because common side effects are fluid retention, feeling bloated, temporary weight gain, and constipation. The amount or length of time laxatives have been used is not always an indicator of how severe the withdrawal symptoms will be.

There's no way to predict how stopping laxatives will affect you. The symptoms may worsen the sensitivity of feeling fat. *Remember that any weight gain associated is only temporary. Symptoms of laxative withdrawal do not lead to permanent weight gain.* Most have symptoms for one to three weeks, although this varies from person to person.

Closing Moments

"No servant can serve two masters" (Luke 16:13).

A successful program and lifestyle is about making the right choices. As we let go of the lies we have believed, forgive ourselves and others, and mend fences, we come to terms with the fact we can eat properly again.

God created so many delicious and exotic foods for our pleasure and nourishment. But we must remember that He created them as fuel so we can function properly. Thank God for your body. He gave each and every one of us an incredible body. Love it and praise Him regularly for it.

Speak it out: "I am made in the image of God!"

Learning to eat healthy is not an end in itself; it's the beginning of more important transformations to come. Make a commitment to take care of yourself. Your body is God's gift to you. Please treat it as one.

Promise to Claim: "I [Jesus] am the bread of life. He who comes to me will never go hungry, and he who believes in me will never be thirsty." (John 6:35)

Week 9

The Road to Damascus

I'm glowing from the inside out!

Before starting this study, we spent too much time focusing on our bodies, on the outside. Now we're starting to see and feel our beauty radiate from the inside. We're headed toward total vibrancy and health. Our faith and healing are not complete until we take what we've learned and experienced and give it to others in need. When God created us in His image, He intended we pour ourselves into one another. That's part of total health.

Do you know a woman or teenager who *never* makes a negative comment about herself? I doubt it, because it's a cultural epidemic. Our mission is to tell others the message about God and His healing power, and show by example how He works.

I've learned that God allows us to go through our life collecting experiences, like bargains at a sale. Then the day comes when we look into our basket of goodies, and we see a whole array of stories and experiences that God has weaved together to be used in our special custom designed ministry.

You may not be called to teach or speak on the subject, but there are abundant opportunities for you to share your message—your story. The gospel of Jesus Christ and your story can build a bridge between you, God, and other people. Remember, God doesn't ask your ability or your inability. He asks only your availability.

Day One: Your Road to Damascus

Ask and seek, and your heart will grow big enough to receive him and to keep him as your own. Wherever God has put you, that is your vocation. It's not what we do but how much love we put into it. —Mother Teresa

Change is the most wonderful part of the healing process.

God works within us to strengthen us, heal us, and make us new. Saul's conversion is an example of such change. We read in Acts 9:1–22 about Saul (better known as the apostle Paul). He grew up trying to follow perfectionism and unattainable standards set by the religious fundamentalists of his day. He thought his salvation was dependent on obeying those standards. His strict adherence to the law and the traditions of the Pharisees led him to throw Christians out of synagogues and have them executed.

It took a dramatic act of God to redirect Saul's passion. While he was on the road to arrest the Christians in Damascus, Jesus confronted Saul. Saul lost his sight and regained it three days later. He then saw the truth. His conversion from religious perfectionism to apostle is an example of the inadequacy of anything that is performance-based.

Like Saul, we've been blind for years, perhaps decades. Now our sight is restored and we're ready for the next step—God's special plan for our lives. He invites us to embrace freedom and a new life. *Today is your road to Damascus experience.*

"I, the LORD, have called you in righteousness; I will take hold of your hand. I will keep you and will make you to be a covenant for the people and a light for the Gentiles, to open eyes that are blind, to free captives from prison and to release from the dungeon those who sit in darkness (Isaiah 42:6-7)."

Day Two: A New Creation in Christ

I tell you the truth, if you have faith as small as a mustard seed, you can say to this mountain, 'Move from here to there' and it will move. Nothing will be impossible for you. —Jesus, speaking in Matthew 17:20

I find it interesting that at AA and OA type meetings the participants identify themselves by their addiction. "Hi, I'm Kim. I'm a bulimic." "Hi, I'm Halle, I'm an alcoholic." As a Christian, I take offense to this. 2 Corinthians 5:17 states, *"If anyone is in Christ, he is a new creation; the old has gone, the new has come!"*

Did you get that? *A new creation!* You are not your disease, or a habit, or what you have made of your life. The following verses describe *who you are in Jesus Christ*:

- 2 Corinthians 3:17–18: *"Now the Lord is the Spirit, and where the Spirit of the Lord is, there is freedom. And we, who with unveiled faces all reflect the Lord's glory, are being transformed into his likeness with ever-increasing glory, which comes from the Lord, who is the Spirit."*

- 1 Peter 2:9: *"But you are a chosen people, a royal priesthood, a holy nation, a people belonging to God, that you may declare the praises of him who called you out of darkness into his wonderful light."*

- Ephesians 1:5: *"He predestined us to be adopted as his sons through Jesus Christ, in accordance with his pleasure and will."*

- Romans 8:17: *"Now if we are children, then we are heirs— heirs of God and co-heirs with Christ, if indeed we share in his sufferings in order that we may also share in his glory."*

This is your real identity. God has given you the highest status in the world! There's no need to wear a mask any longer. You're a child of the King, set apart by God! Being chosen by God means your status, worth, and destiny are determined by Him—not by cultural trends or other people. (And His choosing you was not made on the basis of your social standing, religious practices, or any types of achievement.) How does this make you feel?

For Moms and Role Models

1 Timothy 4:16 says to *"keep a close watch on all you do and think. Stay true to what is right and God will bless you and use you to help others"* (TLB).

If you are a mother, or a role model, or a person who comes into contact with members of the next generation, your realm of influence is great.

Someone said, "Children have never been too good at listening to their elders, but they've never failed to imitate them." You've probably heard the saying, "Monkey see; monkey do" and "Like mother, like daughter." Albert Schweitzer said, "Example is not the main thing in influencing others. It's the only thing." Many adults don't even realize they are a role model of negative body image. When kids hear you complain and pick yourself apart, or criticize others, they begin to believe they must be inadequate.

Monitor the messages you send your children about your own self-worth. I believe when we criticize ourselves we're telling God He's done a crummy job. Paul said, *"Who are you to criticize God? Should the thing made say to the one who made it, 'Why have you made me like this?'"* (Romans 9:20, TLB).

Day Three: A Light of the World

The only ones of you who will be truly happy are those who have found and learned how to serve. −Albert Schweitzer

You have been created for God. And God is love.

This is why you are here—to be loved by God and love Him in return. Everything He's done, He did with you in mind—from creation to redemption. *Redemption* means we've been bought out of sin and slavery (bondage). We were bought with Jesus Christ's blood, not gold or silver, but blood. When we comprehend this sacrifice, and how much God loves us, we want to change. We begin to give of ourselves. We don't live for *self* anymore. Oswald Chambers wrote,

> "The whole human race was created to glorify God and enjoy Him forever. … The purpose for which the missionary is created is that he may be God's servant, one in whom God is glorified. When once we realize that through the salvation of Jesus Christ we are made perfectly fit for God, we shall understand why Jesus Christ is so ruthless in His demands. *He demands absolute rectitude (righteousness) from His servants, because He has put into them the very nature of God."*[36]

God has certain expectations of His children. Romans 2:19 says, "You are a guide for the blind, and a light for those who are in the dark."

Give Back God's Love and Help Others

Jesus says to you,

> *"You are the light of the world—like a city on a hilltop that cannot be hidden. In the same way, let your good deeds shine out for all to see, so that everyone will praise your heavenly Father"* (Matthew 5:14, 16).

You may be thinking that the world is so big and your light so small and unimportant. Nothing could be further from the truth. A wise person once said that to the world, you might be only one small person, but to one person, you just might be the world. We can all light something each day. Perhaps the only thing a person needs is your gift of a smile.

Here are two important starting points:

- *Find a healthy church community.* We all want a church where we feel welcomed, a place to belong. Equally important is to find a church that nurtures your gifts and allows you to grow and help others.

- *Use your testimony (your story of faith and healing in Jesus Christ).* If you're like me, you probably wish you could edit out the not-so-nice chapters of your life. Yet our stories are a picture of God working everything for good. I believe God expects us to use our stories to further His kingdom. But remember, we are still beautiful unfinished projects to God (Philippians 1:6). Our stories won't remain static—they will continue to be altered.

When I first decided to "come out" and share my story it was hard. I soon realized if I shared my story and secrets I could help others break free from their compulsive, addictive behaviors. I also knew God didn't expect me to reveal *every* secret.

Revelation 12:11 says we overcome our enemy by the blood of the Lamb and by the word of our testimony. Contrary to what the devil says, there's power in your testimony! Satan will not be happy with you for tempting to free his captives with your voice of hope. He'll try repeatedly to get you to fall again. Don't get discouraged! Put your armor on every day. Add prayer and practice. God will use you at the right time, in the right place for His glory. Your testimony will shine.

My greatest rewards have come when I've focused on inspiring others and pointed them to God. We all want to know that when we struggle we're not alone in our fears, our sorrows, our defeats, and our hopes. If you ask God to use you to encourage someone else with your testimony, He will (*See Appendix C: How to Write a Powerful Testimony*).

Day Four: God's Plan

Success is what you do for others. –Danny Thomas

We were so certain we knew what was best.

We thought our motives would guarantee happiness. Did any one of us expect to be reading this book or participating in a support group? We expected to have children by a certain age, a particular kind of spouse, a certain career. Did we really anticipate this? Addiction, obsessiveness, and then freedom from it weren't part of the deal. *But it does fit into the big plan!*

Can you now say the joy you feel today doesn't compare to what you anticipated when you started this study? Would you agree that happiness is a choice?

God has healed and delivered me from multiple addictions. No longer the victim, He gave me something no other person could—real freedom. I became *a victor—a survivor*. I knew whatever other problems I'd face He'd be there to get me through. Seeking God with all my heart. I asked Him what He had in mind for my life. Instead of telling the Lord where I wanted to be, I asked Him to place me where I'd fit in, where I was needed. I found *complete peace* after I found His plan for my life . . . and He didn't send me out to a mission field in Africa (most Christian's biggest fear)!

In the classic movie, *It's a Wonderful Life*, George Bailey discovered his destiny. Though he had many opportunities to pursue his ambitions elsewhere, George remained in his community and was dedicated to providing affordable housing to its members. When his guardian angel showed him what the town would be like if he'd never been born, Bailey realized how much of a difference his giving had made. George also discovered another secret—*that what you give is what you receive.*

When you extend yourself to nurture the spiritual growth of another, you nurture your own growth. Although his material possessions were modest, George was toasted the *richest* man in town. Later he remarked, "No man can be poor as long as he has friends." George gave of himself for the joy of giving. Joy is what he received.

By following this path, we too can be blessed. When we remain committed to Christ, abounding in His work, God uses us to change the course of history as we follow Him and obey. Then others turn to Him.

Staying Rooted

God intends to use us to persuade others to change their direction, drop their differences, and enter into His work. He has the power to take our mustard seed faith and move mountains. Our only responsibility is to remain focused on Him and confident in Him. Psalm 1:1–3 says,

> *"Blessed is the man who does not walk in the counsel of the wicked or stand in the way of sinners or sit in the seat of mockers. But his delight is in the law of the Lord [the Bible], and on his law he meditates day and night. He is like a tree planted by streams of water, which yields its fruit in season and whose leaf does not wither. Whatever he does prospers."*

It is comforting to know we're God's workmanship, created in Christ Jesus to do good works, which God prepared in advance for us to do (Ephesians 2:10). Let's remain committed to letting our light shine before others, that they may see our good works and glorify our Father in heaven (Matthew 5:16).

Day Five: Footprints

> *Do not follow where the path may lead. Go instead where there is no path and leave a trail.* –George Bernard Shaw

Serving God is only a small repayment for God's gift of healing. I can tell you firsthand, knowing your purpose will give meaning to your life. Be ready to receive the gifts of God and be prepared for new ones. One of the greatest gifts God gives us is choice. Ralph Marston wrote,

"The footprints you leave behind show clearly where you have been. Yet they do not dictate where you can now go. Perhaps your life up to now has been difficult and filled with disappointment. None of that matters when it comes to the choices now available to you. At this moment in time, you can go in any direction you choose."[37]

Errors and mistakes are the necessary steps in the learning process. They serve a purpose, but they should be left behind. Look back at your footprints and decide where the next set will lead. Your possibilities are limitless as you take God's hand.

Helping Others with Emotional Eating

If you know or suspect someone else close to you is struggling, go to God first. It won't help the situation to force the person to eat or not eat. Here are some suggestions.

- The mean age seems to be going down for the onset of emotional eating disorders. *Early referral* is essential to keep cases from becoming chronic. An important first step is to get *good information*. Don't ambush the person with well-meant but overly direct or critical questioning. Hang in there and have hope. Eating disorders are tough but beatable.

- *Avoid engaging in power struggles over food.* Individual foods should not be labeled "good" or "bad." All foods are neutral.

- *If you are concerned about negative eating behaviors, talk.* Pick a time when the person can focus on the conversation.

- *Educate.* Body image is only a small piece of who we are. We must understand that our bodies are much more than "eye candy." Fat cells are the body's fuel storage tanks, created to be one of the human body's major survival mechanisms. Body fat is normal and necessary to keep skin and nerves functioning. It makes menstruation and pregnancy possible. Strong muscles are essential, which too often are mistaken for fat.

- *Explain genetics.* Despite our culture standards, nobody has a "perfect" body. That would mean they have a perfect genetic code. If Mom and Grandma have pear-shaped bodies, most likely Daughter will too. She'll never physically look like an ultra-thin supermodel. Sadly, fat cell distribution is an inheritable trait.[38]

- *Don't compare.* Any kind of rivalry has the potential to increase behaviors such as perfectionism.

- *Emphasize fun and fitness rather than competition and slimness* if the person is involved with sports or exercise activities. Be aware if their activity level increases suddenly.

- *Professionals say "toss the scale."* The number is meaningless. For years, I gave that number the power to set my mood for each day.

- *Personalize Psalm 139:14:* "I am fearfully and wonderfully made!" That sounds good, but what does *fearfully made* mean? It means there is awesomeness in the way I am made. We are stamped in God's image; therefore, we're to hold ourselves up in reverence and with great respect. Tell her often, "You're beautiful no matter what you look like." This will make a difference.

For a list of more red flags, dos and don'ts, and other valuable information on emotional eating disorders, visit *OliveBranchOutreach.com.*

Closing Moments

The finish line is in full view. Celebrate!

> "Celebration is a high form of praise, of gratitude to the Creator for the beauty of God's creation. To celebrate is to delight in the gift, to show gratitude."[39]

Take the time to delight in your growth, your new relationship in Christ, and your success. Celebrate who you are now—a beautiful, spiritually healthy, delightful, joyous child of God; no longer shackled by the need to be better, perfect, or something you're not. Your beauty shines from within, a radiant glow countless others don't have.

God never gives up on making something beautiful and magnificent out of our lives. Complete restoration still waits us in eternity, yet we can live whole and free and healthy on this earth.

Promise Fulfilled: I [*God*] will repay you for the years the locusts have eaten-- the great locust and the young locust, the other locusts and the locust swarm-- my great army that I sent among you. You will have plenty to eat, until you are full, and you will praise the name of the LORD your God, who has worked wonders for you; never again will my people be shamed. Then you will know that I am in Israel, that I am the LORD your God, and that there is no other; never again will my people be shamed. (Joel 2:25-27)

Final Words from Kimberly

"Do not let this Book of the Law depart from your mouth; meditate on it day and night, so that you may be careful to do everything written in it. Then you will be prosperous and successful." –Joshua, speaking in Joshua 1:8

Healing is active and ongoing. As we proceed along the path of healing, we must make ongoing commitments to increase our faith and understanding of who God is. Commitments include developing a stronger relationship with God, relying daily on the Word, and going to support and Bible study groups or counseling. If we don't devote ourselves to these commitments, our progress will be blocked.

Pray for courage and wisdom to make and maintain positive commitments. Put your armor on every day and be ready to fight back with "It is written . . ." Remember, you're forgiven and deeply loved. There will be challenges ahead along with many blessings. Keep the words of Zephaniah 3:17 close to you,

> *"For the Lord your God has arrived to live among you. He is a mighty Savior. He will give you victory. He will rejoice over you with great gladness; he will love you and not accuse you. Is that a joyous choir I hear? No, it's the Lord himself exulting over you in happy song" (TLB)."*

The road to spiritual growth and transformation has only just begun. I'm overjoyed that you chose to take this journey with me. I want to help and support you as you continue to move forward.

Connect with Kimberly

For a comprehensive list of resources, including counseling and treatment centers, visit my website: *OliveBranchOutreach.com*.

If you want to connect with Kimberly, you can through her website at *www.OliveBranchOutreach.com* or on Facebook. Or, email her at *kim@kim-davidson.com*. She'd love to hear from you or meet you at a future event.

Other Books by Kimberly Davidson

The Perfect Counselor: *Break Through Your Past to Ensure a Healthy Future*
(Some chapters in The Perfect Counselor are also in Dancing in the Sonshine)

I'm God's Girl? Why Can't I Feel It?
Daily Biblical Encouragement to Defeat Depression & the Blues

Dancing In the Sonshine (Second Edition)
Restoration from the Wounds of Abuse
(Some chapters in The Perfect Counselor are also in Dancing in the Sonshine)

Something Happened On My Way to Hell
Break Free from the Insatiable Pursuit of Pleasure

Breaking the Cover Girl Mask: *Toss Out Toxic Thoughts*

Deadly Love: *Confronting the Sex Trafficking of Our Children*

Foundations
Empowering Youth to Establish Healthy Sexuality & Relationships
(A Parent's and Youth Leader's Guide)

Torn Between Two Masters
Encouraging Teens to Live Authentically in a Celebrity-Obsessed World

Appendix A

I Feel Chart

HOW DO I FEEL RIGHT NOW?

Aggressive | Angry | Anxious | Ashamed | Bashful | Bored | Cautious

Confident | Confused | Curious | Depressed | Determined | Disappointed | Disbelieving

Disgusted | Ecstatic | Embarrassed | Enraged | Envious | Exasperated | Exhausted

Frightened | Frustrated | Grieved | Guilty | Happy | Hopeful | Hurt

Indifferent | Interested | Jealous | Joyful | Lonely | Loved | Loving

Miserable | Optimistic | Overwhelmed | Pained | Puzzled | Regretful | Relieved

Sad | Satisfied | Shocked | Shy | Smug | Sorry | Stubborn

Stupid | Surprised | Suspicious | Thoughtful | Withdrawn

Appendix B

I Want an Eternal Relationship with Jesus!

I trust you feel God's unconditional love and you're thirsty for more. I urge you to give yourself up to God so He may do in your heart what you've long desired but failed to do on your own.

Jesus spoke of going to His Father's house and said the disciples knew the way there (John 14:1-4). If we truly desire a personal relationship, now and forever, with God we must know God's address and the best route to get there. How do we reach Him? The answer: through His Son, Jesus Christ.

Jesus said, *"I am the way and the truth and the life. No one comes to the Father except through me"* (John 14:6). There's no such thing as a 12-step program in God's world. There's just one step—accept Jesus Christ as your Lord and Savior. Only Jesus can fill us with a sense of belonging like we've never known before.

If you feel uncertain or unworthy of God's love read Romans 5:8 and personalize it: *"God demonstrates his own love for us* [you] *in this: While we [you] were still sinners, Christ died for us* [you]." Jesus came and died so you *"may have life, and have it abundantly"* (John 10:10). Do you realize that if you were the only person in the world Jesus would have died just for *you?*

Come just as you are—you don't have to be healed, perfect, or addiction-free. Today, by faith, invite Jesus Christ into your life. He said, *"If anyone is thirsty, let him [her] come to me and drink. Whoever believes in me, as the Scripture has said, streams of living water will flow from within him"* (John 7:37-38).

Jesus invites you to partake in the abundant life He offers. If you don't feel ready, you can come back when the Holy Spirit prompts you to. Eventually, a time will come when you'll want to give Him complete control. Pray,

"God, I do believe Jesus is your Son, and that He died on the cross to pay for my sin, and then rose three days later. Forgive my sin and make me part of your family. I acknowledge I've been living separated from you. I now pledge to turn from living my own way. Thank you for this gift, for eternal life, and for your Holy Spirit who has now come to live in me. In Jesus's name, Amen."

If you prayed this prayer God's power has joined you to Christ in a vital, unbreakable, spiritual union. The heartbeat of the risen Jesus beats within you. He's *in you* and will do what no human being can do!

- *"Everyone who confesses openly his [her] faith in Jesus Christ—comes from God and belongs to God"* (1 John 4:2, MSG). "*. . . God has made you also an heir (Galatians 4:7).*
- *"The word of God lives in you, and you have overcome the evil one"* (1 John 2:14). Notice the verse says "you have." This is a present tense promise.
- 1 John 4:4 says, *"You, dear children are from God, and have overcome them* [anti-God lying spirits of the world]; *because greater is He who is in you than he who is in the world."* You are united to the One who is truth!
- *"Because of our faith, he has brought us into this place of highest privilege where we now stand, and we confidently and joyfully look forward to actually becoming all that God has had in mind for us to be"* (Romans 5:2, TLB). In God's eyes, you're now righteous—perfect before Him. And Psalm 1:6 says, *"the LORD watches over the way of the righteous."*
- You've been forgiven for every past, present, and future sin (Isaiah 6:7).

Can't stop eating? Christ can. Can't stop dieting or exercising excessively? Christ can. Can't stop focusing on your flaws? Christ can. The chains of your past and destructive behaviors are broken. *You have a brand-new life ahead of you*!

Appendix C

How to Write a Powerful Testimony

Moving forward means telling your story at some point; reading the chapters that have been written. That doesn't mean you are being called to speak to an audience. God will use your honesty and vulnerability about your experiences to not only continue the transformation process, but strengthen the faith of others.

For some this may be an exercise of confession. Let me assure you that you are not the only one in your particular predicament. The truth is, secrets only hold their power when they're hidden. Once revealed in the light of God's love, they lose their power. Dr. Robert McGee wrote, "Some people hide their prior conflicts better than others, but most of us have ugly stories to tell if we are honest enough to share them."

1. A testimony declares: "I was, but God did, and now I am." In other words, "Death became life, darkness became light, and pain became glory."
2. Read the Apostle Paul's testimony in Acts 26 for a strong example.
3. When you are ready to begin pray and ask the Holy Spirit to direct and counsel you, to bring to your mind what He wants you to reveal.
4. Then write out your answers following this 5-part outline. Give just enough detail to arouse interest, not a blow-by-blow description of every incident. Use these questions to prod your memory. Don't write your story by following and answering the questions. It will sound scripted.

Before: Think about your life before you met the Lord. Your goal is to simply tell what your life was like before you surrendered to Christ. Use these questions to begin molding your story:

*   What was going on in your life leading up to your conversion?
*   What were you searching for before coming to know Christ?

- What problems or needs were you facing at the time?
- How did your life change after that?
- What problem or strong emotion, attitude, or concern were you dealing with? For example, the need for love and acceptance, fear, shame, anger, an obsession, or an illness, loss, or addiction.
- How did you satisfy your inner needs such as loneliness, fear, shame, insecurity? (Ways you may have filled those needs include: work, money, drugs, food, relationships, church activities, the Internet, sports, or sex.)

Describe your new spiritual experience (your born-again and conversion experience). Use illustrations which will cause the listeners to desire this same relationship. Take time to identify the steps that brought you to the point of trusting Christ. Simply tell the events and circumstances that caused you to consider Christ as the solution to your searching.

- Where were you? What was happening at the specific time?
- Did anyone or particular problem influence your decision?

Incorporate Scripture: What Scripture verse or passage or Bible story comes to mind as you meditate on your experience?

Your life today: Describe how your life in Christ is different now. Include illustrations of what God is doing in your life today.

- How is Christ meeting your needs?
- What does a relationship with Him mean to you?
- How has His forgiveness impacted your life?
- How have your thoughts, attitudes, and emotions changed?
- What ministries are you involved in?

Share the prayer of salvation. If you feel led by the Holy Spirit lead the person or audience in the prayer of salvation (see *Closing Moments: Week One*).

Keep in mind:

- *Stick to the point.* Your conversion and new life in Christ should be the main points.
- *Be specific.* Include events, feelings, and personal insights that clarify your main point. Put an emphasis on feelings and emotions

experienced, rather than the experiences themselves. This makes your testimony tangible, something others can relate to.

- *Be honest.* Don't exaggerate or dramatize your life for effect. The simple truth of what God has done in your life is all the Holy Spirit needs to convict others of their sin and convince them of His love.

Words to avoid. Stay away from "Christianese" or "churchy" phrases unless you can explain them. These foreign words can alienate listeners or readers and keep them from identifying with your life. Avoid using these words:

- **Born again, conversion, or regeneration.** *Instead use:* spiritual birth, spiritual renewal, become alive spiritually, given a new life.
- **Saved.** *Instead use:* rescued, recovered, found hope for life, healed, delivered from despair, danger, or suffering.
- **Lost.** *Instead use:* heading in the wrong direction, going down a road to nowhere, separated from God, had no hope, depressed.
- **Gospel.** *Instead use:* God's message to man or the good news about Christ's purpose on earth.
- **Sin.** *Instead use:* rejected God, in a power struggle with or fought God, missing the mark, going down the wrong path, broke God's law, disobeyed God.
- **Repent.** *Instead use:* admit a wrong, changed my mind, heart and attitude completely, made a decision to turn in the other direction, turned around 180 degrees from what I was doing.

Notes

[1] Volkow, N. 2002. 'Nonhedonic' food motivation in humans involves dopamine in the dorsal striatum and methylphenidate amplifies this effect. *Synapse, 44* (3), 175-80; Volkow, N. 2008. Inverse association between BMI and prefrontal metabolic activity in healthy adults. *Obesity, 17* (1), 60-65; Volkow, N., & Wise, R. 2005. How can drug addiction help us understand obesity? *Nature Neuroscience, 8* (5), 555-60; See also Louden, K., "Refined Carbs May Trigger Food Addiction," July 9, 2013, "Effects of dietary glycemic index on brain regions related to reward and craving in men," Am J Clin Nutr. September 2013.

[2] Stated by Dr. Linda Mintle in her presentation, "Make Peace with Your Thighs: Overcoming Food Addiction," *AACC Counseltalk;* October 16, 2012.

[3] Lisa Harper, "Blessed Are the Desperate," *Bible Gateway NIV Devotions for Women*, July 18, 2013.

[4] See Acts 5:3-4; Psalm 139:7-8; 1 Cor. 2:10-11. The Holy Spirit is indeed a divine person because He possesses a mind, emotions, and a will. He thinks and knows (1 Corinthians 2:10); can be grieved (Ephesians 4:30). He intercedes for us (Romans 8:26-27), makes decisions according to His will (1 Corinthians 12:7-11).

[5] See Isaiah 49:14-15, 18; Jeremiah 24:7; Matthew 23:37; Mark 12:29-30; Matthew 22:36-38.

[6] Oswald Chambers, *My Utmost for His Highest, January 19*, Vision and Darkness (Uhrichville: Barbour and Company, 1963).

[7] Gregory L. Jantz, *Hope, Help, and Healing for Eating Disorders* (Wheaton: Harold Shaw Publishers, 1995.) 63.

[8] Quoted in *Women's Devotional Bible* (Grand Rapids: Zondervan, 1995), 524.

[9] Valerie Whiffen, *A Secret Sadness,* (Oakland: New Harbor Publications, 2006), 1.

[10] Drs. Larry Crabb & Dan Allender, *Hope When You're Hurting* (Grand Rapids: Zondervan, 1996), 105–107.

[11] *The American Heritage Dictionary of the English Language, Fourth Edition* (Houghton Mifflin Company, 2000).

[12] Paraphrased, *Screwtape Letters* by C. S. Lewis: Severson, Beth Donignon. *Women's Devotional Bible 2, NIV* (Grand Rapids: Zondervan, 1995.), 1274.

[13] A. W. Tozer, *Tozer Topical Reader*, comp. Ron Eggert, 2.185, Camp Hill: Christian Publications, 1998.

[14] Gregory L. Jantz, *Hope, Help, and Healing for Eating Disorders* (Wheaton: Harold Shaw Publishers, 1995), 101.

[15] Charles Stanley, *In Touch*, January 2005, Atlanta: In Touch Ministries, 7.

[16] See Deuteronomy 22:28-29; Exodus 22:16-17.

[17] Sheila Walsh, *The Heartache No One Sees* (Nashville: Thomas Nelson, 2004), 173.

[18] Jantz, Gregory L., *Hope, Help, and Healing for Eating Disorders* (Wheaton: Harold Shaw Publishers 1995), 125.

[19] Neil Anderson, *The Bondage Breaker* (Eugene: Harvest House, 2000, 2nd Rev.), 69, 72.

[20] Marilyn Meberg, *I'd Rather Be Laughing* (Nashville: Word Publishing, 1998), 128.

[21] Used by Permission: *The Voice of the Martyrs*, htttp://www.persecution.com.

[22] Drs. Frank Minirth, Paul Meier, Robert Hemfelt, Sharon Sneed, *Love Hunger Workbook* (Nashville: Thomas Nelson, 1991), 210.

[23] Gregory L. Jantz, *Hope, Help, and Healing for Eating Disorders* (Wheaton: Harold Shaw Publishers, 1995), 15.

[24] *Serenity Prayer:* written by Reinhold Niebuhr, July 1, 1943 for the Union Church of Heath, Mass. It is used in Twelve Step programs today.

[25] Permission to reprint granted by Gregory L. Jantz; "Real Solutions for Regaining Control," *Christian Counseling Connection*, Volume 19, Issue 1; p. 12, 2013.

[26] Pope Gregory the Great, 6th-century a.d., first listed the seven deadly sins. The seven deadly sins, also known as the capital vices or cardinal sins, are a classification of vices used in early Christian teachings to educate and protect followers from basic human instincts; Accessed 05–20–2006, http://en.wikipedia.org/ wiki/Seven_deadly_sins

[27] See: http://www.brainyquote.com/quotes/keywords/sins.html.

[28] Gregory L. Jantz, *Hope, Help, and Healing for Eating Disorders* (Wheaton: Harold Shaw Publishers, 1995), 141.

[29] Valerie E. Whiffen, *A Secret Sadness*, (Oakland: New Harbor Publications, 2006), 39.

[30] Patrick Quillin, *Healing Secrets From the Bible*, (The Leader Company, 1995), 5.

[31] Gregory L. Jantz, *Hope, Help, and Healing for Eating Disorders* (Wheaton: Harold Shaw Publishers, 1995), 96.

[32] Gregory L. Jantz, *Spiritual Path to Weight Loss* (Guideposts Books, Lincolnwood: Publications International, 1998), 11.

[33] See http://www.livestrong.com/article/297851-visualizations-for-weight-loss/#ixzz2XqEsa2vE.

[34] MacRae, P., et al. 1987. Endurance training effects on striatal D2 dopamine receptor binding and striatal dopamine metabolites in presenescent older rats. *Psychopharmacology, 92* (2), 236-40.

[35] Women's Body Image, National Women's Health Information Center, 1–800–994–9662, available from http:// www.4woman.gov; accessed 6 November 2004.

[36] Oswald Chambers, *My Utmost For His Highest, September 21* (Uhrichville: Barbour and Company), 1963.

[37] Ralph Marston, *The Daily Motivator*, http://www.greatday.com; accessed August 2004.

[38] Stated in: Drs. Frank Minirth, Paul Meier, Robert Hemfelt, Sharon Sneed, *Love Hunger Workbook* (Nashville: Thomas Nelson, 1991), 266.

[39] Melody Beattie, *Live It Up! Recovery Devotional Bible* (Grand Rapids: Zondervan. 1993), 330.

Made in the USA
Columbia, SC
21 June 2017